The Nicene Creed

Ancient Words in the Light of Modern Faith

Martha Porter

ST. JOHANN PRESS

Haworth, New Jersey

ST. JOHANN PRESS

Published in the United States of America
by St. Johann Press
P.O. Box 241
Haworth, NJ 07641
www.stjohannpress.com

The paper used in this publication meets the minimum requirements of the American National Standard for Information Sciences—Permanence of Paper for Printed Library Materials, ANSI/NISO Z39/48-1992

Interior design and composition by Susan Ramundo (susan@srdesktopservices.com)

ISBN 978-1-937943-01-1

Manufactured in the United States of America

Contents

Acknowledgments

This collection owes a particular debt to three historians of the church—Joan Chittister, Luke Timothy Johnson, and Richard Rubenstein. Their excellent overviews and analyses of this period of the church's history have refreshed and expanded my knowledge and understanding, providing both general contexts and specific commentary that have been a major resource.

Having engaged in theological education and teaching for over twenty years, it is sometimes difficult to attribute the source of one's knowledge. Every effort has been made to do so, not only to give credit where credit is due, but to share the many writings that have been valuable to me over the years in the hope that they can be resources for others as well.

I treasure my family and friends who gave encouragement and support through their responses to the book. Particular gratitude goes to Barbara Wendland, who was willing to review this manuscript and saw enough potential to connect me with Dave Biesel and St Johann Press, who made it a reality.

Preface

Sometimes I am asked which books were most influential for me during my seminary education. It's an easy question to answer, for the two books which fit that criterion still occupy a place of honor on my bookshelf, some 30 years later. Their interiors are colorful, with multiple underlines, marginal notes and stars in red, green, blue and yellow, almost as if they had been illustrated. Their soft covers are creased at the spine and frayed at the corners, smudged with what might be a bit of grease from late night pizzas. The books are Peter Berger's foundational work, *The Sacred Canopy,* and a slim volume by Gordon Kaufman titled *An Essay on Theological Method.* They were, and are, important because they changed the way I looked at the world. They are not "easy reads" but they are well worth the effort involved in digesting their contents.

Both offer an analysis of the ongoing human process of building social structures in secular as well as religious arenas, with a focus on the powerful role that language can play in this endeavor. Berger outlines distinct steps or stages of the construction: first is *externalization,* the outpouring of our creative efforts; second, he describes *objectivation,* in which the created object or structure takes on a certain factuality or "givenness;" then he shows how we move to *Internalization,* as those created structures or norms act back upon us. One of the concluding steps is *legitimation,* in which the institutional or social structure is undergirded by an authority, ranging from the parental "because I said so" to "and God said. . . ." Finally, there is *alienation,* whereby we "forget" our part in the continual creative process that structures and maintains our world. (1)

Language itself is one of the human constructs that Berger uses to illustrate this process, saying that we "... invent a language and then find that both our speaking and thinking are dominated by its grammar." (2) From a more theological, but yet congruent perspective, Kaufman proposes that "... the language we speak provides a principal foundation for our religious experience. ..." (3) He even declares that "... without those symbols to guide our consciousness, these 'experiences' would not be available to us at all." (4) If we accept the validity of the process described by Berger, and the centrality of language that both men point to, we would see what we say, and the kind of world we thereby put in place, as crucially important.

This process occurs throughout our culture; we can see it in something as straightforward as the system of signals we have devised to manage traffic, where "red" and "green" take on much more meaning than is inherent in their colors, and we all know what it means to "give the green light" to a project. We can feel how this created norm acts back upon us as we ponder whether to go through a long red light at a deserted intersection. We do not give time to wondering how the world might be if red meant "go" and green meant "stop." The system has become a given, legitimated by the authority of the law. Of course, any traveler to other parts of the world quickly discovers that there are other norms, other "givens," some of which appear to be just short of chaos. Those people who drive on "the wrong" side of the road, or mingle cattle with cars, would be just as disconcerted by our systems.

Whatever systems we function within on a day-to-day basis are mostly necessary; we cannot reinvent the world each day. We need humanly constructed, stable systems of commerce, education, justice, and others. The problem arises when we become so alienated from the fact that all these systems are a product of human creation, and we lose the ability to adapt, to change, to grow, and to correct or reconstruct systems which are oppressive and discriminatory.

We can see this process of alienation functioning with peculiar power in the words laden with tradition and empowered by their association with the Holy, the words we use in worship, the words which Berger says offer the most powerful legitimation possible—we do this or don't do that because "God" says thus. For example, when the more or less final draft of The Nicene Creed had been voted on, the emperor Constantine is reported to have said, ". . . the decision of 300 bishops must be considered no other than the judgment of God." (5)

The Creed was both a religious and a political tool, a humanly constructed statement of belief that gave order and meaning to the world of its time. The question this book raises is whether it still gives order and meaning to our world—or rather, what *kind* of order and meaning does it give to our world? In the following pages, the Creed is examined phrase by phrase—first, to help us *wake* up from our alienation, to be aware of the very human constructive process which brought it into being, and the legitimations which have kept it in place all these years; and second, with an awareness of the constructive part we play, to give thought to how we find order and meaning in our world today, and the language we would use to convey that.

As you read the reflections on each phrase, give thought to how it functions for you. What would you gain through an awareness of your part in this constructive process? What might you lose? For there are losses as well as gains—stepping out of systems which have been a given all our lives means "growing up," leaving behind a sheltered "crib" which has defined our world with limits we could not even put a name to, could not question because they have been so consistently and powerfully legitimated. Even though these structures are limiting, we rely on them because they create a measure of comfort and security. Outside the "crib" there is freedom and risk—freedom to explore, freedom to make choices, to discover new dimensions of your self, and new ways of naming what you choose to call Holy. The risk? For some of the writers of the Creed, there was a risk to life and limb. For us it is more likely to be feeling the loss of the familiar, facing the challenging work of reconstruction, while the theological house that has sheltered us lies in ruins. Sometimes relationships are put at risk. Sometimes social or professional acceptance.

Is it worth it? You decide.

Introduction

The "Amen" has been sounded to the sermon. Like a puppeteer, with a twist of his wrist the priest motions the congregation to its collective feet—and then, "We believe . . ." The Creed begins, with a murmur that spreads quickly to every pew, every throat, every corner—or at least, most.

We all say the same words—but do we give them the same meaning? As the voices join in to repeat these ancient words, some hear the reassuring ring of tradition; some hear lilting magnificent poetry; some use its words to speak their own beliefs; for others it defines their faith and binds them in community.

But there are those for whom the time-worn words hold little meaning and the poetry is bare cover for a theology they have long abandoned. They stand silent at certain passages or mumble the words. They do NOT believe; they have questions, and they feel alone in the crowd of worshipers.

The metaphors in the Creed *work* for some people. They have been so legitimated, so integrated with the other components of worship, that the possibility of change or challenge is at minimum unsettling to some and almost horrifying to others. Whether these worshipers know of the statement or not, they would agree with Emperor Constantine that the Creed devised by the bishops was nothing less than "the judgment of God."

For others, however, those for whom the Creed feels more like a constraint than a confession of faith, an awareness of the steps in world construction described by Peter Berger can loosen the confines of the language of the Creed, with the reminder that world creation is an ongoing process in which they can participate. They can "deconstruct" the metaphors and "construct" new ones that speak more meaningfully to their experience of the Holy.

Some of the questions that will be part of the process are:

Where did the Creed come from? Who wrote it? When? Why?

To search for answers to these questions about the formation and history of the church is to enter a world that makes what we might today call "dirty politics" look sophomoric. When the nature of God is being defined, the stakes are high and the results have ultimate implications. Indeed, the words of the Creed have been dearly bought. The historical considerations here will not be comprehensive, nor necessarily sequential, but rather linked to specific phrases within the Creed as they seem to illuminate choices or bring a sense of the struggle to our awareness.

Is it beautiful poetry, or an outdated formulation? Does the lilt of the words add to or obscure its meaning?

Is it an individual or communal statement? What was its function when it was written?

And, as you personally reflect, what in the Creed is central to your faith? Are there parts you would rather not say? What would it mean to change it? Or sometimes use other statements of faith, other creeds? How would your worship be affected? Would you see God or your self differently?

Dedication

I think it is true to say that, almost without exception, every lecture I have attended for the last 18 years—including Marcus Borg, Barbara Brown Taylor, John Dominic Crossan, John Shelby Spong, Joan Chittister, and others—has included the same question from some member of the audience. That question was "What do you do about the Creed? Can you say it? Do you cross your fingers?"

This collection of meditations on the Creed is dedicated to those questioners, and to the Contemporary Theology Class at The Church of the Incarnation, Highlands, NC, which has raised questioning to a fine art and an act of faith.

The Nicene Creed

We believe in one God,
the Father, the Almighty,
maker of heaven and earth,
of all that is, seen and unseen.

We believe in one Lord, Jesus Christ,
the only Son of God,
eternally begotten of the Father,
God from God, Light from Light,
true God from true God,
begotten, not made,
of one Being with the Father.
Through him all things were made:
For us and for our salvation
He came down from heaven:
by the power of the Holy Spirit
He became incarnate from the Virgin Mary,
And was made man.
For our sake he was crucified under Pontius Pilate;
he suffered death and was buried.
On the third day he rose again
In accordance with the Scriptures;
he ascended into heaven
And is seated at the right hand of the Father.
He will come again in glory to judge the living and the
dead, and his kingdom will have no end.

We believe in the Holy Spirit, the Lord, the giver of life,
who proceeds from the Father and the Son.
With the Father and the Son
he is worshiped and glorified.
He has spoken through the Prophets.
We believe in one holy catholic and apostolic Church,
We acknowledge one baptism for the forgiveness of sins.
We look for the resurrection of the dead,
and the life of the world to come. Amen.

In learning about the Nicene Creed, you might remember some of the following:

1. That it was written by a Council of Bishops meeting in Nicaea in 325 A.D. True
2. That the Council was called together by the Roman Emperor Constantine, newly converted to Christianity. True
3. That it brought unity to an empire and a church threatened with division. Sadly, not true.

The years following the formulation of the Creed by the Council of Bishops were torn with political maneuvering, exile, excommunications, intimidation, torture, violence, and murder. All of this mayhem was supposedly done in the interest of securing the correct definition of the nature of the relationship between Jesus and God, and creating a peaceful and unified empire and church.

History suggests that ambition and a craving for political and ecclesiastical power played a part, as well as theological convictions. Some of the major players—Alexander, Arius, Athanasius, Eusebius, Constantine—could be ruthless in their pursuit of the goal of theological triumph. The initial consensus ". . . at the Council of Nicaea was, in large part, an illusion. . . ." writes one historian. "There were lessons to be drawn from this experience, but few had learned them. Consensus cannot be created by verbal formulas. Serious disputes are seldom resolved without a genuine change in the parties' thinking. And a false consensus may be more productive of conflict than an honest disagreement." (6)

It surely was a false consensus if the following years of conflict are any evidence.

A closer look at the Creed and its history may give us insight not only into the past, but also into our present. Though we might disavow the violence which accompanied the Creed's development, we can hardly say that violence "in God's name" is a thing of the past. Temples, churches and mosques are still sometimes the target of choice when a difference carries theological overtones. Tensions in personal as well as community relationships are still generated when we face theological differences. We find "honest disagreement" hard to talk through, hard to live with.

Writing of his experience with such conflict, Robert Jensen notes:

"We live in a world awash with debate about religion, spirituality, and faith that often seems to derail rather than deepen our quest to understand the world in which we struggle to live fully and responsibly. The problem is not the clashing of ideas; such clashes often advance knowledge. Nor is the problem that such debates can be on occasion sharp-edged and tense; such edginess is common, maybe inevitable, when people disagree about important issues. The problem is simply that the conflict is rarely constructive." (7)

We disagree.
Can we talk?
If you believe *that* . . . you're not a Christian
Can we talk?
If you don't believe *this* . . . you're not a Christian.
Can we talk?
What is there to talk about?
How much I love you

"We believe . . ."

What we know as the Nicene Creed had its roots in an ancient Jewish confession of belief known as the *Shema: "Hear O Israel, the Lord our God is one God . . . (Deut. 6:4)." (8)*

With the beginning of the Christian experience through the life and teachings of Jesus, and the subsequent genesis of the church in all its many forms, this foundational confession demanded some elaboration that would clarify the relationship between Jesus and the *"one Lord"* of the Shema. By the fourth century, the theological battles were raging in earnest. The conflict centered in Alexandria.

Alexander, the bishop in Alexandria, and his assistant and eventual successor, Athanasius, saw it as crucial that Jesus be affirmed as fully human AND fully divine. Arius, a persuasive and personable priest, argued that, while Jesus was indeed divine, he was also human in a way that made him unequal with the Father, the God of Creation. Alexander insisted that Jesus was coeternal with the Father, but Arius contended that there was a time when Jesus was not. Both clerics were capable of moving from persuasion to force to make their point.

The dissension in the Christian community over these definitions was intense and divisive enough to threaten not only the stability of the church, but also the unity of the Roman empire itself, then ruled by the Emperor Constantine, a recent convert to Christianity. When Constantine convened the famous Council of Bishops in Nicaea to formulate a statement of belief, he hoped that it would resolve the differences and unify both church and state.

The creed which emerged from this gathering succeeded only in intensifying the theological conflict within the church. Despite the state "seal of approval" on the Creed from Constantine, who wrote, ". . . *the decision of 300 bishops must be considered no other than the judgment of God,*" (9) the debates escalated from disagreement to violence.

The Creed ultimately may have given the emerging church an identity that allowed it to survive, but it could not then and has not now unified Christianity around a single understanding of who Jesus is in relation to God—much less who God is. In spite of this, Christianity has been and remains a religion heavy on right belief—hence the beginning of the Creed—*We believe. . . .*

Though it was perhaps fashioned as a confession of the church rather than an individual affirmation, many people experience it as an insistence to give individual consent to the definitions and premises of the Creed— even if these are less than clear.

The feeling often is that one must say *"I believe . . ."* if you are to be a member of the community that says *"We believe. . . ."*

Well-handled words,
debated,
disputed,
denied,
affirmed,
fashioned to
capture the Christ
who comes to us
yet eludes us.

Is it poetry,
theology,
history,
heresy,
a ticket to be punched?

Notes

Notes

"... in one God ..."

The world into which Christianity was born had a multiplicity of gods, each of whom had a role in the well-being and fate of the state, the rulers, and the people. This panoply of gods included the imperial rulers, to whom god-like status was attributed. One historian has noted that the religion of that era functioned more at a national or social level, with personal, individual meaning found in philosophy or the mystical religions (10) .

With Emperor Constantine's conversion to Christianity, the church could more fearlessly affirm a belief in God, and specifically a belief in "one" God. In the various times that Christians experienced persecution, they were urged to acknowledge other gods, not necessarily *instead* of their "one" God, but in *addition* to. For those steeped in the traditions of a multiplicity of gods, a loyalty unto death to "one" God must have been hard to fathom.

Today our continuing affirmation of one God may be an accurate reflection of what we believe in our minds, but close observation of what we do sometimes offers a contradictory picture.

In a Sunday morning church class in Christian parenting, which drew a group of about 30 people, parents were asked to make a list that was titled, "What I wish for my children." Predictably the lists included admission into a good school, health, security, safety, professional success, a strong family life—all things that any loving parent would hope for. For the second assignment, they were asked to turn the paper over and make a list titled "What God wishes for my children." These lists were considerably shorter, but took much longer to complete.

As we talked, it became obvious that the first list was truly a list of their "gods"—what they gave priority to, what they valued and invested time and resources in, where their hopes were grounded. The second list surfaced not only a different set of hopes and dreams, but the possibility of struggle and even disappointment on the way to acquiring what God might wish. Words like love and wisdom and faith showed up. But no one wanted to dispense with their first list. No one wanted to make a commitment to "one God" and "one God" alone—to risk having their child not get into that prestigious school, or carry on the family banner of success, or find the perfect spouse, the fulfilling job. It was difficult to even think of letting go of other gods, of giving your whole heart, not to mention the life of your child, into the hands of the "one God."

There's the
"parking space god," the
"shopping god," the
"money god," the
"green light god," the
"promotion god," the
"tenure god," the
"big enough house god," the
"beauty/handsome god." the
"my child will be successful god," the
"good health, I will live forever god," the
"golf/football/basketball/whatever the season is god."

Which god do I believe in today?

Notes

Notes

"...the Father, the Almighty..."

These words selected by the bishops carry a lot of freight.

1. They begin to identify the role of the "one God" as part of a trinity (that puzzling Christian mathematics);
2. they speak to the potential of a personal, even parental, relationship with God;
3. they reflect both scriptural and cultural norms which speak of God as Father;
4. they reinforce the hierarchy that dominated both religious and secular aspects of life in that era;
5. and they give the broadest scope possible (the Almighty) to God's power.

There are those for whom these words, and the image they invoke—God as an all powerful Father—stir warm memories of their own loving father who, through his presence, made the world a secure and trusted place.

But there are also those for whom these words evoke memories less reassuring—they recall a father who was critical, absent, unpredictable, even abusive—a father who, through his presence and his power, made the world a painful and frightening place.

Any personification of God is immediately beset with memories and feelings from life experience. This holds true in those instances when, in an attempt to introduce equity, God is named as Mother as well as Father.

So what to do? Do we ignore the pain stirred by the words for those with sharp-edged memories of Father? Do we attempt a dubious equity, calling God Mother? Do we bind ourselves to images in scripture, seeing those as the only legitimate options? Do we introduce contemporary terms with meaning for today's searching Christian? Do we speak of this one God as Creator, Friend, Healer, naming other varieties of relationship without gender or power issues?

In a creatively illustrated book titled *In God's Name*, (11) the people give different names to God which are based on their varying experiences of the sacred—the names include Shepherd, Peace Maker, Rock, Redeemer, Comforter, as well as Father and Mother. In the end, the people join their voices together in calling God by every name, and as their voices blend, they call God "One."

Once upon a time,
with the heat of a burning bush
reddening his face,
the barefoot stranger,
instead of presuming to name you,
and yet needing credentials,
asked your name.
The reply that came was:
"I am who I am."

Not satisfied,
we have given you many names,
each one breaking off a piece of "I am",
each one creating the illusion that
we have the power to name.

Best we learn to say for
our own selves: "I am who I am,"
and turning, hear the call to
stand barefoot before
the mystery of simply being.

Notes

Notes

". . . maker of heaven and earth . . ."

There is blood on these words—and fire.

The framers of the Creed wrote in a time when the Ptolemaic vision of heaven and earth was dominant—the earth was seen as the center of a closed universe, unique in its creation by an all powerful God.

It would be almost 1200 years before another vision was proposed by Copernicus, as his observations, without even a rudimentary telescope, brought him to conclude that the sun stood still, and the earth moved around it.

Those who followed in his path encountered the wrath of the church. One of those was Giordano Bruno (1548–1600), who adopted the Copernican view, and advocated freedom of thought and religious tolerance. This cost him dearly; he was convicted of heresy by the Inquisition of the Roman church, imprisoned, tortured, and finally burned at the stake in 1600, but not before "his jaw was clamped shut with an iron gag, his tongue was pierced with an iron spike, and another iron spike driven into his palate." At his sentencing, Bruno said, "In pronouncing my sentence, your fear is greater than mine in hearing it." (12) Little wonder that his fellow scientist, Galileo, under pressure from the church, in 1633 renounced his belief in a Copernican universe.

But the proverbial cat was out of the bag. In the words of Goethe: "Of all discoveries and opinions, none may have exerted a greater effect on the human spirit than the doctrine of Copernicus. The world had scarcely become known as round and complete in itself when it was asked to waive the tremendous privilege of being the center of the universe. Never, perhaps, was a greater demand made on mankind—for by this admission so many things vanished in mist and smoke! What became of our Eden, our world of innocence, piety and poetry; the testimony of the senses; the conviction of a poetic-religious faith?" [This new doctrine] ". . . authorized and demanded a freedom of view and greatness of thought so far unknown, indeed not even dreamed of." (13)

Though we have probed our corner of the universe with telescopes, with satellites, with the lonely explorers launched into oblivion beyond our solar system, though we now have achingly beautiful and humbling images of what lies beyond our minuscule planet, though we have begun to track the history—and even the future—of the universe since its moment of inception, we still face formidable limits in our knowledge of what constitutes "heaven and earth."

Writing in *The Luminous Web* , Barbara Brown Taylor notes that "no one knows exactly how old the universe is, how big it is, or how quickly it is expanding. And no one can say who lit the fuse in the first place. However far back science is able to go, there is always the problem of a first cause. How does something come from nothing? How can there be a bang without a match?" (14)

A fuse—a match—
our minds stumble at "nothing",
living as we do
immersed in so many "somethings".
The proposition now afloat is
that there are other universes.
We are not only not the center,
we don't even have a starring role in all there is.
Living into that mystery makes the
mind buzz, grow still,
draw back to what we state as certain,
fasten the gate against the intruding fear

that we, like any dust speck,
will be casually dusted off one day

Impelled by that fear, we have lit our matches,
not to create universes,
but to burn questioning flesh.
Even now, the fires are being lit for those
who ask the questions today.

Notes

"... of all that is, seen and unseen ..."

Some historians of the church suggest that this phrase was included in the Creed to rebut the lingering influence of the theology propounded by Marcion, (85–164 A.D.). He was born into a Christian family and became ". . . a wealthy man, a ship-owner and merchant whose businesses took him about the Mediterranean and to Rome." Following a dispute with the churches in Asia Minor, where he was denounced as "the first born of Satan", he settled in Rome, initially finding acceptance. But after writing a work he titled *Antithesis,* he was excommunicated. What made him so controversial?

Marcion separated the God of the Old Testament and the God of the New Testament—the first was the source of the physical world, with all its finiteness and failings, while the second was the ground of a spiritual world, characterized by "love, boundless peace and serenity." In striving to live into this spiritual vision, Marcionites rejected the secular world and its institutions, including family—they were ascetics who sought salvation through individual purity. (15)

The bishops, with this language, affirmed that all that is seen—that is, the physical, material world and the natural laws which govern it—as well as that which is unseen—the spiritual world—emanate from the same One God.

In our world we must bridge the two, for physicists are discovering more and more about the invisible building blocks of our visible world. The concept of tiny particles that make up all matter was first proposed by a 5th century B.C.E. philosopher named Leucippus. He even called them "atoms" from the Greek word for "indivisible. (16)

Do you remember the first time you heard the word "atom"—that infinitesimally tiny scrap of matter that echoes our solar system with its nucleus of protons and neutrons and its ever revolving electrons. Many of us heard it first in relation to another word—bomb—and the injunction to crawl under your wooden school desk for protection when the air raid siren sounded. How could something so small be so powerful?

Today the world of physics is shot through with words which try to name the invisible (quarks, strings, black holes) and the formulation of theories about their qualities and how they function.

Our journey into the invisible world is a bit like Gulliver's travels—we are helplessly large creatures trying to find our way among the most minute but yet powerful elements. If it is true, as theorized, that the observer always changes the observed, we must proceed with caution and awe, for we might yet undo ourselves completely. These ventures into the world of the unseen, the invisible, offer us new ground upon which to explore our spirituality. They also offer the temptation to exercise powers for which we clearly are not ready—see above, on the protection offered by a wooden school desk.

The sirens sound;
in the classrooms startled looks
etch the faces of children
crawling beneath their desks,
breathing in the dust
tracked in from playgrounds
now deserted.

The all clear sounds,
relief dawns,
the visible world resumes its pace;
for today the invisible world
has been held safe in God's hands.
What about tomorrow?

Notes

Notes

"We believe in one Lord, Jesus Christ . . ."

Remember the "Christian mathematics?" In this phrase, which leads us into the heart of the Creed, we see the culmination of long debate and much dissension, even violence, over whether "one plus one equals one" or "one plus one equals two." Here the bishops begin to define who Jesus is in relation to God.. "The problem that neither side in the controversy had yet grasped was this: whoever presented a detailed explanation of the relationship of the Father to the Son could fairly easily be accused of heresy. This is because it was difficult, perhaps impossibly so, to describe Jesus' relationship to God in a way that did not seem either to deny his humanity . . . or to question his divinity. . . ." (17)

But first to the word "believe." Marcus Borg has elaborated on the implications of this word by contrasting the difference between "I believe you" and "I believe *in* you." "I believe" implies an acceptance of a particular something as truthful—"I believe you will be home on time." The latter phrase—"I believe *in* you"—however, is not about the factuality of something, but about the more general qualities of trust and faithfulness— "I believe in you"—I trust that you will come home every day, that you have a commitment to our relationship.

Borg also explores the etymology of the word "believe," and in its Old English derivation finds a link to the word "love," so that "believe" in translation has the implication of "be love." Our confession is that we "believe *in*"—that we "be-love" this Jesus, who is Lord. (18)

These meanings can gain ground only with distance from the politically charged Council of Nicaea, where history seems to tell us that "believe" did indeed mean assent to the factuality of something. Lack of assent was likely to get you excommunicated from the church, at minimum, and in some instances, beaten senseless or killed. In the ongoing competition to define the critical points of Christian theology, over the years other councils were held, other views expounded, and other creeds formulated. The Council of Chalcedon in 451 A.D. produced the Athanasian Creed which proclaimed that "this is the catholic faith, which, except a man believe faithfully, he cannot be saved." (19) To the participants, there was always much at stake in these theological battles.

Are we called to "believe" the propositions of the Creed about the one Lord, Jesus Christ? Do we give our mental assent to the intricate webs of theology that have been spun across the years? And if so, to which one?

Or do we "belove" the one Lord, Jesus Christ, because of his life, because of his passion for justice, because he could see into the human heart, and because he seemed to have a habit of eating with the most unseemly people, which might just include us?

Believing,
my mind interviews
the theologian for
"Just the facts, thank you,
And take your time, This is quite intricate, and
after all, there is much at stake."

Beloving,
my heart stays painfully open
to the woman camped on the street,
to the immigrant worker living
in the trailer without water,
to the family stopping at the food pantry.
After all, there is much at stake.

Believing—beloving ??

Notes

Notes

". . . the only Son of God . . ."

Two words—"only Son." They slip off our lips so easily, and we forget, if we ever knew, that it took the intervention of the Emperor of Rome to settle on them.

"Only"—In a time when some rulers still claimed divine origin and status, and there were multiple gods populating the heavens, to say that Jesus was the "only" Son of God was to directly challenge established mores and power structures. It was a political as well as a theological statement. The bishops wanted to assert what they saw as the truth: "that Christ came from and returned to God in a way that no other human has or will or could. . . ." (20)

"Son" Since the bishops were writing retrospectively, they knew the person who was the subject of the Creed was male. Hence, the "Son." But what did "son"-ship imply to them?

There were certainly those who took more of an "adoptionist" stand, saying that God adopted Jesus as His son at his baptism, with the words "This is my beloved Son, in whom I am well pleased." Others saw an implication of subordination, as a human son is subordinate to his father, not as powerful, not as wise, not ready to be in charge, but having to grow into that state. But for others, "son" carried the conviction of an identity with God—just as a human child is "flesh of my flesh and bone of my bone," so Jesus as God's son was of the same substance as God. And as we shall see, that identity did not begin at some point in time, but was true for eternity.

But what if . . . ? What if something different had happened when Mary's child was born? A Christmas sweatshirt available in some catalogs is printed with a colorful nativity scene. The caption above it proclaims in bold print, "It's a girl !!" In her book, *To Love Delilah*, Mary Cartledge-Hayes imagines that possibility. The same flow of events begins the story—the visitation by the angel Gabriel, sharing the news with Joseph, the journey to Bethlehem, the shepherds, the wise men, the stable, the star. But in this story, the shepherds and wise men found Joseph striding out of the stable, vowing that he had nothing to do with either the child or the woman. When they spoke to Mary in praise of her child, the Son of God, she replied, "God is here with us incarnate, but my child is not the Son of God. She is the Daughter of God, sent to cleanse us of our sins and lead us to the life everlasting."

The wise men and shepherds withdrew to consider this, then gathered their companions and began to depart. The final shepherd to leave hurled a torch into the stable, and the flames rose to the star above.

The world sank into darkness.

After many generations, God, in great wisdom, sent another child to the weary earth. This one's name would be Jesus. He, at least, would be permitted to speak." (21)

What if . . . Mary's child had been a daughter? How would you write the story?

Being the only, younger daughter
in the household with
an only, elder son,
she learned her place—
and that was barely beyond notice
until she did something
worthy of the anger that swirled
through the house, anger that
one day lit her own fire,

a fire that blazed into a passion
to be more, rather than always less,
to be whole, rather than fragmented,
to be the bearer of possibility,
to know her body to be the body of Christ,
her self, the presence of Christ.

Notes

". . . eternally begotten of the Father . . ."

"Begotten"

Do you remember high school English? If you were transported there, and the teacher asked you to define "past participle," could you do it? I couldn't—not without looking it up. Which I did, in this case.

Past participle—a word formed from a verb and used as an adjective.

"Begotten"—past participle of "beget".

And what does "beget" mean? To produce a child, or cause to happen, from the Old English "get, or obtain by effort."

Sometimes the words we choose have meanings which are not immediately apparent, even to those choosing them. With "begotten," the meaning most of us might think of first would be "to produce a child." We sometimes refer to the genealogies in the Bible as "the begets" or "begats" as child after child and generation after generation are named.

Though it is difficult to know exactly what connotations that word had in 325 A.D., we can say with some assurance that the primary purpose of the word in that context was to assert that Jesus was of the same essence or substance as God—not that God "birthed" Jesus," but that God "caused Jesus to happen."

Now the dilemma. A birth, or even something that happens, is to us an event and implies a time dimension—it happened yesterday, it happened last year, it happened a long time ago, it will happen next week. If Jesus was "begotten", or birthed, or caused to happen, there might logically, to the human mind, be a time before that event—a time when Jesus was not. But if Jesus was to be equal with the Father, then there could not be a time when he was not—it wouldn't look good on his resume to have missed out on some foundational events, perhaps.

Therefore, the inclusion of the word "eternally." Just as God was eternal, and there was not a time when God was not, so with Jesus. Though "begotten," he was somehow "eternally begotten."

The Creed contains eight different, overlapping descriptions of how, in fact, Jesus is divine and has the same divine standing as God. If we encountered such redundancies in secular writing, our fingers might itch to hit the "delete" button. Another option is to put alongside the Creed of 325 A.D. a new voice in today's church which invites us to define less and love more.

You, O God, are infinitely generous,
good beyond all measure.
You came to us before we came to you.
You have revealed and proved
your love for us in Jesus Christ,
who lived and died and rose again.
You are with us now.
You are God. (22)

Notes

Notes

". . . God from God, Light from Light, true God from true God . . ."

It is here in these lines that the theological warriors find their muse. With the rhythmic ring of poetry, the bishops reiterate the nature of Jesus—he was God from God, Light from Light, and if there was any doubt, true God from true God.

Though still directed at theological distinctions about Jesus—was he truly, wholly divine—this sidestep into poetic form stops the arguments for awhile. You can debate a definition based on rational or logical approaches, but not poetry. Poetry is directed to a different part of your brain, to your emotions, to your unconscious. It is like the hymns sung since childhood, whose words can be recalled by aging minds that have forgotten familiar faces, or even their own face.

Returning to the distinctions made by Marcus Borg between "I believe" and "I believe in," we might ask which way of believing is addressed by the more poetic form in these lines. Does the form obscure the meaning or illuminate it? Does the lilt of the words discourage delving into their history and meaning, because beauty will be lost in such an endeavor? Or is there an invitation to ride the words like the hawk rides the wind to a meaning that ultimately is beyond words?

Though we must confess the beauty and mystery in these words— God from God, Light from Light, true God from true God—they can leave us with a Jesus who is just as invisible or hidden as God. What are we believing—who are we believing in? God from God, Light from Light, true God from true God—or the Jewish itinerant preacher with dusty feet and an open heart?

John Shea, in *The God Who Fell from Heaven*, turns the power of poetry to shape an image of God with us.

If you had stayed
tightfisted in the sky
and watched us thrash
with all the patience of a pipe smoker,
I would pray
like a golden bullet
aimed at your heart.
But the story says
you cried
and so heavy was the tear
you fell with it to earth
where like a baritone in a bar
it is never time to go home.
So you move among us
twisting every straight line
into Picasso,
stealing kisses from pinched lips,
holding our hand in the dark.
So now when I pray
I sit and turn my mind
like a television knob
till you are there
with your large, open hands
spreading my life before me
like a Sunday tablecloth
and pulling up a chair yourself
for by now
the secret is out.

You are home. (23)

Notes

Notes

". . . begotten, not made . . ."

"... then God said, "Let us make man in our own image, according to our likeness . . ."

Genesis 1: 26

... then the Lord God formed man from the dust of the ground, and breathed into his nostrils the breath of life; and the man became a living being . . .

Genesis 2:7

The centrality of the theology regarding the divinity of Jesus is evidenced by its repetition. The fourth century theologians, as well as those who preceded them, saw human salvation as dependent on Jesus. More specifically, they saw salvation as dependent on Jesus' full divinity and oneness with God, for otherwise he would not have the power to save. Therefore, the division between those who argued for full divinity, and those who saw Jesus as the pinnacle of humanity, was deep and conflicted.

They drew upon the events of the Genesis story which were clear—God *made* man—in God's image and likeness to be sure, but nevertheless formed from dust and dependent on God for the breath of life. The human beings so created were clearly different from and subordinate to the Creator.

Jesus, however, in the Creedal language, was not *made*, but *begotten*—God *caused him to happen*—and his full divinity was assured, and affirmed in this statement of oneness.

These are not debates we are likely to hear repeated in the 21st century. Our language is still trinitarian, and Jesus is still God's son, but the range of theological perspectives stretches more comfortably from Handel's *Hallelujah Chorus* to *What a Friend We Have in Jesus*. We are more likely to identify with Jesus' humanity, so achingly rendered in the lyrics of the song, "One of Us", written by Eric Bazilian and originally released by Joan Osborne. (24)

Imaging the more human aspect of the incarnation, she sings:

What if God was one of us,
Just a slob like one of us,
Just a stranger on the bus,
trying to make his way home,
just trying to make his way home.

Even Jesus asked the question of his disciples, "Who do you say that I am?"

"Who do you say that I am?"

Careful.
It's a pop quiz.
Did you do the assigned reading?
You have ten minutes,
then put your papers on my desk.

Here's a secret though—
if you didn't do the reading,
(and truth be told, it wouldn't do you any good),
look out the window,
see the haze, the hint of color in the woods;
look around you,

see the person next to you,
their brow furrowed with concentration
erasing the two lines they just wrote;
see life, curled in the twigs, waiting to burst,
see life, breathing two feet away.

Now put that on paper.

Notes

". . . of one being with the Father.
Through Him all things were made."

I remember as a kid in elementary school (a long time ago), that when we talked in class, passed a note to our best friend three rows over, or got the unexplainable and irrepressible giggles, our teacher would make us stay after school and write on the board some version of:

"I will not talk in class."

what seemed like a thousand times, but may have been just 50 or 100.

There are points at which The Nicene Creed takes on the same feel. We have
the only Son of God
eternally begotten of the Father
God from God
Light from Light
true God from true God
begotten, not made,
of one being with the Father.
(*And finally . . .*)
Through him all things were made.

Somewhere we pass from assurance to protestation—as in "The lady (or gentlemen, in this case) doth protest too much, methinks." The comment by Queen Gertrude to Hamlet, when understood within its context of

Shakespearean England, means that someone "*affirms* so much as to lose credibility. . . . [The] vows are too elaborate, too artful, too insistent." (25)

Perhaps the bishops gathered this collage of images about Jesus because they had spiritually, and sometimes even literally, staked their lives on the truth of them. They had to make sure that every possible attack upon the divinity of Jesus could be rebuked—*no*, Jesus as son was not subordinate; *no*, there was not a time when Jesus was not, *no*, God did not "make" Jesus as God made humankind, *no*, Jesus was not just "like" God but rather the same as God.

The possibility that these elaborations could have gone even further is recorded in a history of the early church, where Constantine's son, who succeeded him after his death, is described as "mean, suspicious and petty. . . . His desire to maintain religious unity degenerated into a pedantic search for minute formulations which could be imposed." It was said that he "confused the Christian religion which is plain and simple, . . . and fogged issues which were perplexing enough in themselves . . ." (26)

The only words
worth repeating
over and over and over:

I love you.
I forgive you.
I miss you.
Come home.

Notes

Notes

The relationship between Jesus and God was at least tenuously defined, but still debated by those who thought him fully divine and those who argued for some conditional terms. Constantine himself was torn between the two sides, and many ". . . found themselves drawn first to one side, then the other—or, to end this troubling uncertainty, found themselves violently affirming that one side was in sole possession of sincerity, fidelity, and the truth." (27)

But now the turn was to the nature of the relationship between Jesus and *humankind*. Why would God choose to become incarnate, take on human form? What, in their understanding, was the purpose? How was such a thing accomplished? What could it mean?

The turn from "Jesus the same as God"—eternal, begotten, true God—to "Jesus the man" was an intricate maneuver. Arius and his followers in the East gave emphasis to Jesus as the perfect human, who was "promoted" or "adopted" to his divine status. But the western bishops who agreed with Alexander and Athanasius on the full divinity of Jesus were determined to insure that the Creed did not imply that the humanity of Jesus in any way subtracted from his equivalence with God.

That these definitions were shaped by the cultures in which they arose is a given. And the plural—cultures—was the case. Geographical, intellectual and philosophical differences created dominant and distinct regions—the Latin West and Greek East. In one history of the period, the regions were characterized thus:

"Among the Latin bishops there was a great suspicion of the overly clever Greeks, with their tendency to produce novel combinations of Christian and Platonic ideas. Western churchmen had not been persecuted to the extent that their Eastern brethren had, but they toiled in a rougher physical and social environment, less urbanized, more exposed to barbarian threats and incursions, and less completely Christianized. These beleaguered clergymen had little taste for high-blown theory and no sympathy at all for Eastern attempts to qualify the divinity of Jesus. The Christ they preached to their ex-pagan congregants was God on earth, period—and if this produced difficulties for some Middle Eastern intellectuals, so be it." (28)

Each camp had their own worldview—as we have ours. And ours is no more uniform than theirs was—truth be told, it is probably more widely diverse than can be adequately described. We too have our East—more urban, industrial, full of history and tradition—and our West—more adventurous, laid back, unconventional, and exploratory. What Creed could span this gap, as well as taking the middle into account?

Today
when tolerance is more in fashion,
when the invitation is to mystery
rather than certainty,
when we embrace doubt
at the same time we look for hope,
when the Council of Now has gone for the day,
and we're picking up trash in the great hall,
we let the silence speak
and there find a hand to hold in the dark.

It is enough.

Notes

Notes

". . . for us and for our salvation . . ."

About forty miles east of our town is a small red brick church tucked into the curve of the road. A grassy bank partially shields it from sight and muffles the traffic noise. Embedded in the bank is a sign carefully crafted from large wooden logs painted a bright red. The sign declares, "JESUS SAVES."

Though I pass it by in less than a second, the message stays with me and I wonder about the congregation. A visit there on a Sunday morning would no doubt include a warm welcome, and coffee and cookies in the fellowship hall after the service. But somewhere, somehow, sometime, before the exit could be gained, a question would be posed: "Are you saved?", or, "Have you accepted Jesus as your personal savior?" There would be an accompanying assurance that giving my heart to Jesus would secure my future in heaven and rescue me from the torments of hell.

The Christian citizens of the Roman empire in the fourth century were already giving less and less thought to the historical Jesus, the Jewish rabbi "who walked the earth, then died and returned, and who would soon come again to inaugurate his Kingdom." That image ". . . was fading into the background like a figure in an antique mosaic . . ." as the years passed and being replaced by the "internalized Jesus: that is, the image of Christ that people would keep in their minds and hearts . . ." (29)

"Neither paganism nor Judaism made the possibility of eternal life the centerpiece of its thinking. Christianity did. . . . Amid general fears of a social collapse, one could nurture the radical hope that unpredicted change might be vastly for the better instead of for the worse. . . . On the individual level, it was clear that ordinary people could become new men and women in Christ. . . .

Either/Or. On one side, unprecedented dangers; on the other, dazzling hopes. Either believe rightly, act righteously, and be saved, or fall into error, sin and be lost." (30)

Saved from what? Saved to what? Saved in the here and now? Saved in the hereafter? Our modern world view, which cannot place heaven or hell in the "above" and "below" regions they previously occupied, questions the meaning of salvation. Like our sisters and brothers in Christ from the fourth century, we have a multiplicity of images and options from which to choose. Unlike our fourth century siblings, we have rejected, at least intellectually, the either/or option. A translator of the Benedictine pattern of spiritual living even advises, "Quit the search for salvation; it is selfish." (31)

"Don't be scared . . . don't be scared"
is the resurrection chant of the preacher.
But it's too late,
for fear long ago curled itself and
settled in the marrow of my bones,
to be wakened by the smell of sweat
and sawdust, by the sound of
creaky organs and pounded pianos,
sounding "you are lost" louder than any
note of grace that might be shimmering
in the stars.

The love eludes me, washed as it is
in blood and guilt. The only grace
I know seems to come at the cost of my soul.

The chanted words of grace ("don't be scared . . .")
scatter like seeds, take hold in my head,
do their best on rocky soil.
My heart as yet
holds no fertile ground.

But still I wait—still I listen, and hear the echo . . .
"don't be scared . . ."

Notes

". . . he came down from heaven . . ."

In the still blackened theater, people began to fumble for their coats and make their way toward the exit. We sat stunned, unmoving. Our only comment to each other was , "Wow!" Slowly we gathered ourselves, our coats and the empty popcorn bags and emerged into the busy lobby from what had just become one of our favorite movies. It was 1998 and the movie was "The Truman Show."

If you have seen it, no words of explanation are necessary. If you have not, words are barely adequate. In the movie, a world is created that may just be a close parallel to the literal everyday conception of the universe in the fourth century—the earth is sheltered under the dome of the heavens, and even the possibility of movement outside the dome brings the threat of chaos and death. Most chilling is Christof, the character above the dome, who choreographs the life of the main character, Truman. Christof exercises a God-like omnipotence and omnipresence and is willing even to sacrifice the man who he says is like a son to him in order to maintain control.

When Truman discovers that he is living in an artificially created serene world, he gathers his courage and chooses to leave. His breezy but courageous farewell comment to the creator of his world is the habitual greeting he gives to his neighbors: "If I don't see ya, have a good afternoon, good evening, and good night." With that he steps into the unknown, outside the dome, challenging Christof's contention that we "accept the reality of the world with which we are presented." Like the story of Adam and Eve, Truman's curiosity leads him out of the garden to engage in the fullness of life.

We cannot know for sure how the fourth century people conceptualized the world, and how literally they interpreted the reality, presented to them by their senses, of an alternately blue or black dome, lightened by one major light and many minor lights.

Wherever heaven was, whatever heaven was, IF heaven was, they surely thought of it as a place or a way of being that was serene, and untroubled by the same concerns that confronted them in their fragile and unpredictable world.

To state that Jesus came "down" from "heaven" was not only to point once again to his divine source, but to claim his transformative presence in the here and now of experience in the world.

Whether "down" and "heaven" imply spatial movements and realities, or are purely metaphorical, they communicate a presence that is "here" rather than "there," "close" rather than "far," more like us than not like us. One can imagine as Jesus prepares to leave the perfection of "heaven" and come "down" to earth, a wave of his hand and the words, "If I don't see ya, have a good afternoon, good evening, and good night." And then the step, not into a scripted reality show, but into the unknown that each of us must face.

The story says that God chose—
chose to pour God-self into flesh
for the sake of our souls,
for the sake of our hearts,
for the sake of love.

Love is not good at making plans.
Love just opens its arms.
Sometimes it's met with an embrace.
Sometimes with nails.

No telling how this would all turn out.

Notes

Notes

". . . by the power of the Holy Spirit . . ."

Here the third member or aspect of the Trinity is introduced. There is no definition given at this point, no clarification of a relationship to God, the Father. There is only the attribution of power—the *power* of the Holy Spirit.

Earlier or alternative versions of the Creed, while it was still in the process of development, are crafted differently. An initial proposal at the Council of Nicaea was a creed in use in the church of Eusebius of Caesarea; it read simply ". . . who was made flesh for our salvation. . . ." There was no mention of the Holy Spirit or Mary. A first revision still mentioned the incarnation only in passing—". . . was made flesh, and became man, . . ."

The version which finally bore the name "The Nicene Creed" had been amplified and edited in councils which met in 381 A.D. and in 451 A.D. There was still no mention of "power," but the Holy Spirit was now part of the process. The Creed affirmed that Jesus ". . . was made flesh of the Holy Spirit . . ." (32)

So does all this nit-picking about language have any meaning? In her book, *Loving the Questions*, Marianne Micks reminds us that this is theological language, not biological language. (33) But to learn that words are powerful and can create unintended associations, one has only to listen to women who have experienced rape and other kinds of violence. The "power" of the Holy Spirit, as described in the nativity story of the Gospel of Luke, is a "power" that "will come upon you, and . . . overshadow you". Such language is disturbing to victims of violence, so much so that one woman's startling assessment was, "Sounds like rape to me."

We cannot take too seriously the power and impact of the language we use. Biblical language has a unique power to shape our perceptions of the world and relationships because there is the implication that the world and order portrayed are ordained by God. Thus, in this story, submission before power—Mary's characterization of herself as a servant, and her consent—"Let it be with me according to your word."—create a model for women that is echoed in other portions of the New Testament which call for women's submission to their husbands.

Feminist theologians, both women and men, have written extensively in recent years, reclaiming strands within the Christian tradition which honor women's experience, and developing new perspectives and interpretations that envision the Holy as inclusive of all humanity.

"Then the angel departed from her."

Was it a dream?
A vision?
Joseph?

Whichever—
the curve of her belly,
the tightness in her back,
the heaviness of her step,
the small fists and feet
that pummeled her from inside—
these were real.

Son of God? Holy?
No question he would be her son.
Beloved.

Notes

Notes

". . . He became incarnate . . ."

"Incarnate" comes from the Latin word *"incarnare"* meaning "make flesh." For the writers of the Creed, the God of creation had, in Jesus, become clothed in flesh, embodied. And all this without losing an ounce of his divinity.

Some early Christians thought otherwise—taking a "docetic" view, from the Greek *dokein*—they argued that Jesus only *seemed* to be human—that his humanity was not real. Asked to draw a picture of him, they might draw someone floating just above the earth, never having dirty feet or a tired back, or needing to eat or rest or even take a bath. Being human and being divine were ultimately incompatible. While this view was deemed a heresy by the early church, it can be seen sneaking into our modern vision in the images of Jesus glowing in many a stained glass window—white robe, tranquil smile, halo around his head of perfectly groomed hair.

But those who took the incarnation seriously saw a real human being, an embodied person, with flesh like any flesh—it itched, dried out, sustained cuts and bruises, had imperfections, and felt fatigue and pain. Fred Craddock tells the story of waiting in line at an art gallery to see a new painting of Jesus that was creating a lot of controversy. He was expecting something lovely, but instead encountered a figure that was ugly, disheveled, almost repellant. When he expressed his astonishment, the artist said, "Didn't you know—haven't you read?" "He had no form or majesty that we should look at him, nothing in his appearance that we should desire him. He was despised and rejected . . . a man of suffering and acquainted with infirmity; and as one from whom others hide their faces . . ." (Isaiah 53)

Aside from the mystery about Jesus that is contained in incarnational theology, there is the mystery as well of how it pertains to us. We are embodied creatures who are born, live, and inevitably die. We bear in our bodies all the joys and pangs of life; we are fragile and at the same time remarkably durable and resilient.

We in the church speak of our being the body of Christ—specifically, the body of Christ *for each other*. If that is true, then incarnation is not something that happened once long ago, but something that has the potential to happen, indeed, does happen over and over. With every moment that we are present to each other, when hearts are open and faces lit with welcome, when time is given to listening, when the chair beside the hospital bed is filled with supportive companionship, or the refrigerator stocked with nourishing meals, when a word of encouragement strengthens the spirit—then the body of Christ is incarnate again.

It is not a "spiritual" process so much as it is the reality of presence, the reality of the body in all its beauty and messiness and joy and pain. Frances Frank captures that reality in her brief and graphic poem about the incarnational moments that foreshadowed the Eucharistic words.

Did the woman say?

Did the woman say,
when she held him for the first time
in the dark dank of a stable,
after the pain and the bleeding and the crying,
"This is my body; this is my blood?"

Did the woman say,
when she held him for the last time
in the dark rain on a hilltop,
after the pain and the bleeding and the dying,
"This is my body; this is my blood?" (34)

Notes

Notes

". . . from the Virgin Mary . . ."

If it is not wise to discuss politics and religion over the dinner table, it is particularly disastrous to good digestion to raise the question of the virginal conception of Jesus. Literal belief in a unique event, otherwise considered biologically impossible, has become for some the litmus test of Christian identity, as well as one of the key elements giving divine character to Jesus. No virgin birth, no divine nature for Jesus, no hope of salvation.

Those who espouse a literal, historical event do not easily tolerate a "mythic" interpretation of the conception of Jesus. Nor are they swayed from their perspective by the differences in the gospel birth narratives, or the fact that parallel stories existed to convey the special status of Roman rulers of the time. For them, "myth" equates to false, rather than an alternative way of speaking the truth.

In his epic book, *The Birth of Christianity*, John Dominic Crossan argues that the writers of the gospel birth narratives were not constrained by our rational either/or approach to reality, but rather lived in a world "where divine conceptions were quite acceptable, where, in fact, divine and human, eternal and temporal, heaven, earth, and Hades were marvelously porous and open to one another." Crossan maintains that the claim of a virgin birth was not meant to be a unique claim, but rather a counter cultural claim—God is to be found in Jesus, born a poor peasant child, rather than Augustus, a powerful and fabulously wealthy Roman emperor, whose conception was also characterized as miraculous. (35)

The claim was not so much biological or even historical as it was theological. Here, in this man, not that man, we see God. Here, the face of humility, there, the face of power. Here, dusty feet and sandals, there, flowing robes and a battle shield.

For those who rest more easily with myth, there is the challenge to tell the story in a way that still holds the meaning, that opens a liminal space between our mundane realities and the mysteries that surround us. What we cannot take literally, we must imbue with the truths of metaphor and myth. We must tell the story in a way that speaks to our hearts, that edges around our own brand of literalness, and points us toward the truth held in a star, a stable, and a baby.

She was six, he was seven.
Both stumbled a bit, wrapped as
they were in sheets and dish towels.
The shepherds moved restlessly,
resisting the urge to joust with their staffs,
and the angel was having trouble with her wings.

It was almost time.

The organ began softly,
the familiar tune flowing out among
those gathered.
Lights dimmed.
The shepherds settled down.
One candle, then another, and another.
"Silent night, holy night . . ."

Oh, that it could be—this night, every night—
"sleep in heavenly peace . . ."
Oh, that it could be.

We give light to each other,
feel our throats close on the words,
dab at an unexpected tear,
for innocence, for despair, for hope.

Most surely it is time.

Notes

". . . and was made man . . ."

※

"He had a face . . ." Frederick Buechner says in the opening lines of *The Faces of Jesus*, a collection of images of Jesus from all times and places. Leafing through the weighty book, you meet not one Jesus, but many. There is

. . . Jesus with a broad nose and full lips carved from dark wood by an artist in the Philippines

. . . Jesus frozen in marble, his right hand raised and his shoulders draped in flowing robes, from 13th century Italy

. . . a rotund baby Jesus, held by his even more rotund mother, with a pillow over his head for a halo, from 20th century Uruguay

. . . a serene boy Jesus, with eyes that slant and hands that offer a perch to a white dove, from 20th century Korea

. . . an angular baby Jesus clinging to the bare breast of his angular mother, both painted black with golden hair, from Melanesia

. . . Jesus with a corded whip in his hand, creating chaos in the temple, from 16th century Italy

. . . a distinctly Chinese Jesus, complete with Asian eyes, a mustache and goatee, holding the wafer to be blessed at the last supper

. . . a crucified Jesus, all skin and bones, spikes protruding from his hands, his agony made real, from 20th century Italy (36)

The images begin to blend, not into one man, but into a "human" seen through the eyes of other humans. The experience echoes the assertion that the Creed, in fact, uses the Greek word for "human" in this phrase rather than the Greek word for "man." (37)

The vital issue being decided through the choice of words in the Creed was whether or not Jesus, already declared to be fully divine, was also fully human. In his full humanity, Jesus modeled for all a way of life that enlivens him for us yet. And the use of the more inclusive term of "human" also mirrors the reality that both women and men participate in being the body of Christ for the world today. Perhaps one day an addendum to *The Faces of Jesus* will include the feminine as well as the masculine faces that continue to embody the Christ.

He had a face . . .
Whose dimensions and planes
we can only measure by deeds

He had a face . . .
That glowed with intelligence,
that saw through all the defenses
to the heart of who you are,
that could be tender with compassion,
and grieved at your grief.

He had a face . . .
That would be transformed with a smile,
contented in the company of friends,
but silent before taunts or threats.

He had a face . . .
That held the anxiety and finally, the agony.

Was it brown? Fair? Rotund? Hollowed?
Was it comely or plain?
Was the nose broad or high?
The eyes straight or slant?
The hair light or dark?

Would you see that face—
the face of Christ?

Be brave.
Look in your mirror.

Notes

". . . For our sake . . ."

The implication is one of need—a need that the authors of the Creed say that Jesus answers with himself.

"Sake" is a funny little word. It generally means "in the interest of" or implies a reason for something to be done. It is never used alone—but rather is

for your sake
for the children's sake
for the sake of your country
for safety's sake
for argument's sake

and sometimes, when impatience wins out,

for God's sake!!!

Someone puts their own interests in the background, and gives the interest of someone else center stage. Without debating whether Jesus had a divine commission to do so or not, it is clear that he gave priority to the interests of the people he encountered:

from the need of a short but agile tax collector to see him up close, or

the need of a woman to touch his hem and free herself from exile, or

the need of the community to break out of patterns of fear and submission, or the need of all to see power confronted with truth and the willingness to be faithful unto death to that truth—

all this for our sake.

In our human interactions, hearing the words, "I'm doing this for your sake," can sometimes carry intimations of guilt and conflicted gratitude. But with Jesus, it seems that what he did "for our sake" was as much a full expression of himself as it was something he did for us. He spoke the truth not so much because we needed it but because the truth demanded to be spoken. He healed and touched not so much because we were sick or broken, but because he could not contain the love that lived within him. He faced death and embraced it not because we needed a sacrifice, but because it was the only way he could stay true to himself.

It ended up being "for our sake"—because it called us to live just as fully and faithfully into our own lives as he did into his.

For your sake,
for my sake,
for all of us to have a hope
then
for God's sake
let us fashion a way
of living that is every day
for all our sake.

Notes

Notes

". . . he was crucified under Pontius Pilate . . ."

Appearing in the middle of the Creed, Pontius Pilate is the nail that binds the story, not only to a cross, but to a particular time and place. Ancient histories record his role as governor of Judea from 26 to 36 A.D., and the biblical record makes him a central character in every version of the story of the crucifixion of Jesus.

In the synoptic gospels, when he is confronted with the crowd calling for the death of Jesus, he asks the question, "Why, what evil has he done?" The crowd gives their answer, and the deed is done.

But in John's gospel, a different and memorable question is directed to Jesus: "What is truth?"

Is the question from Pilate a heartfelt search for an answer to his life? Is it a cynical commentary framed as a question? We cannot hear the tone of his voice, or see the curl of his lip to give us a clue. We can only know what sparked his question—the statement by Jesus that he ". . . came into the world to testify to the truth."

That there was a truth to be had does not seem to be in question. But Jesus, having said he came to tell the truth, stands mute at the question. Why? Perhaps because the truth is not a word spoken, but a life lived. It's like the joke explained that is no longer funny. It needed a crowd of motley folk—lepers, cripples, the demon possessed, the poor, the outcast—to bear witness to the truth that was in the life of Jesus and that Pilate could not comprehend. It is doubtful that Pilate gave much thought to the event in the days that followed; it was, after all, just one more crucifixion among many. He could not have dreamed that his name and his questions would come down over the years as central to the story.

Perhaps we should not regard the different accounts of that day separately. Perhaps, taken together, Pilate's questions "Why, what evil has he done?" and "What is truth?" are also nailed to each other—for to some, then as now, to tell the truth is to uncover what we would hide, what we would disown and put onto others, and this leads us toward death and evil, not life and wholeness. Nevertheless, truth telling is rarely welcome, as Jesus and others who followed his path would find.

What is truth?

The impossible for us is
to speak the "TRUTH."
Very occasionally we can manage the "truth;"
but usually we give voice to just our own particular "truth."
Sometimes even that is more than we can bear.
Certainly more than we can live.

But the promise of the one who stood before Pilate
was that there is a truth,
and it is that which glues our feet to
the floor each morning,
and keeps the stars in their places,
and somehow speaks to us
across all time,
bidding us to seek not only
words of truth as we can hear them,
but a life of truth we can follow.

Notes

Notes

"... he suffered death and was buried ..."

I can sing it to you yet, the words are so familiar . . .

On a hill far away, stood an old rugged cross,
the emblem of suffering and shame,
But I love that old cross,
where the dearest and best,
for a world of lost sinners was slain.

In innumerable churches that hymn, and the theology it reflects, have been an integral part of worship over the years. The suffering of Jesus on the cross has often been the cornerstone of a theology that says God (a) requires the suffering and death of Jesus to satisfy the debt created by sin, and/or (b) the suffering is necessary to uphold the moral order of life which is threatened by our offenses. This is an interpretation which relies on the idea of "redemptive violence," that is, that there is violence which serves to redeem or purify the person or the world.

Writing in *The Christian Century*, Daniel Bell states that "all of this is wrong. God does not demand or require blood to redeem us. God neither inflicts violence nor desires suffering in order to set the divine-human relation right. In spite of its pervasiveness in Christian imagery, the cost of communion, of reconciliation and redemption, is not blood and suffering." (38)

The suffering of Jesus has also been employed to convince people who are suffering from life circumstances, including discrimination and oppression, that their experiences are to be embraced as Jesus did the cross. Thus minorities are to endure the degradation of discrimination, and spouses, mostly women, are to endure violence in the home—their suffering will make them like Christ, goes the argument.

Bell proposes an alternative, in which he offers "Christ [as] our substitute **not** in the sense that he takes our place in the execution chamber and suffers our punishment for us, but in the sense that he offers God the fidelity [and] devotion . . . that we should have but did not, and subsequently could not." (39)

It is certainly true that the cross was especially cruel and created unimaginable suffering for the victim. It can remind us of how we cause suffering to others, both intentionally and unintentionally. It can also make us aware of the violence in our words—we engage in a "war on drugs" and wonder why it becomes a real war; we embark on a "war on poverty" and end up blaming the poor for the systems that bind them to defeat.

That Jesus suffered, died and was buried is not in question—only what we make of it. The cost of communion, of reconciliation and restoration, is a nonviolent life, not a violent death.

The old dog shakes from
tip to tail as he emerges
from the river,
joyfully flinging water
from his coat and
bounding away refreshed.

I follow into waters now
turned baptismal,
and feel the encrusted
weight of centuries begin to lift.

On the shore again
I rival the old dog
as I dance,
flinging water from tip to toe.

Notes

Notes

". . . on the third day he rose again . . ."

The quest for the historical Jesus can follow him from birth to death, turning over rocks, dusting for ancient pottery, tracing the paths he took, organizing the multitude of data about the wars and victories and defeats and personalities of leaders, unraveling the issues that seized the attention of first century citizens.

But when we come to this statement in the creed, all the data fall away. There is no archeological dig to bring evidence for or against. This is a faith statement, pure and simple.

Like the virgin birth, it is also foundational for most Christians. Many would say if there was no resurrection, no rising on the third day, then what's all the fuss about. Believe it and you're a true Christian; don't believe it, or even doubt it, and you will find yourself on the outer fringe of Christendom.

For those who experience the Christian faith as primarily *believing* the correct things, the factual Truth (with a capital T) of the resurrection is essential. For those who embrace a Christianity that focuses more on *following* Jesus of Nazareth, what happened or didn't happen on that third day is less important.

Resurrection does not promise immortality, but a return to life after death. There are many things that can die in our lives besides our bodies—hope, love, faith, dreams, relationships. Believing that the resurrection of Jesus happened in a particular way may not guarantee experiencing resurrection in your own life; not believing it doesn't preclude the experience of resurrection in each hour, each morning, each day. When what was dead in us becomes alive, then there is resurrection.

Asked to comment on the Creed, one veteran priest said the following:

"Like the parables, even the whole canon of scripture, we must look through and beyond them to grasp their timeless meaning. The creed is the same. Get too literal with any of this and you will likely find an extreme narrowing of grace.

The true mystery of Judaeo-Christian faith lies far beyond the limits of any human language.

Anyone who hasn't crossed their fingers from time to time is either lying or an idiot.

(And, quoting Tillich), The beginning of faith is doubt."

With these acerbic comments, he challenges the people for whom he is a loving pastor. They love him in return because his own life is revelatory of resurrection.

The fence borders the drive,
marking the way
with posts of locust, newly cut,
grounded in concrete,
surrounded by asphalt.

The rains come;
spring announces itself
once more.

Each post is long
divorced from its home
of rich dirt and companioned trees,
but the warming sun stirs memories,
and small sprouts adorn the posts,
defying the concrete tombs,
giving witness to a persistence
of life that bespeaks
resurrection.

Notes

". . . in accordance with the Scriptures . . ."

When the Creed was being drafted, the early church had barely settled on the books to be sanctioned and included in the canon. Athanasius, key player in the conflict over the Creed, compiled and circulated a list of the books that he thought should comprise a New Testament for the Christian faith, saying of his list, "In these alone the teaching of godliness is proclaimed. No one may add to them, and nothing may be taken away from them." (40)

In that period there was very little critical study of the texts. Origen (185–232 A.D.) did make a study of Hebrews, and he noted internal inconsistencies that led him to reject Paul as the author. Origen's student, Dionysius, raised similar textual questions about Revelation. But the process of academic study and biblical criticism did not begin to emerge until the seventeenth century.

The decision to close that series of statements about Jesus—crucified, suffered, died, buried, and rose again—with the phrase, ". . . in accordance with the Scriptures . . .", indicates that the bishops wanted to declare that what had happened to Jesus was not a defeat, but a part of God's plan for the events of Jesus' life. Like the Gospel according to Matthew, which makes frequent use of the phrase, ". . . all this took place to fulfill what had been spoken by the Lord through the prophet . . . ," the statement in the Creed affirmed that all that had happened was an expression of God's will.

A familiar children's song uses the same device—"Jesus loves me, this I know, *for the Bible tells me so* . . ." It is not unusual to draw upon the authority of the Bible to validate a claim or a decision. Burned into the memory of most Southerners of a certain age is the use of Scripture to justify slavery and continued prejudice and mistreatment of African-Americans. More generally, Scripture is still sometimes quoted to justify the restrictions of equal rights for women and those in the gay and bisexual community.

Modern biblical scholarship, which includes historical criticism, form criticism, literary criticism, and text criticism, has for many altered the way they see the scriptures. They are seen as a human product rather than a divinely inspired one, with valuable truths embedded in their stories, and their prophetic powers attributable to keen insight into human nature. They carry a different sort of power, more related to wisdom than to authority. The childish assurance that rested in ". . . the Bible tells me so . . ." is gone, and the arduous work of finding new meaning has begun.

"The Bible Memory Association" was the definition
of dread for the anxious ten year old,
whose Saturday mornings were marred by
the requirement to memorize and recite the week's
quota of verses. The lure was a new book to read,
picked from the loaded shelves in the cluttered
room where they met, as well as the approval
of that adult world that set the rules.

Now, with books easily acquired with the
swipe of the credit card, and the
literal exchanged for context and metaphor,
there is release, not only from the necessity of
memorizing, but also from the struggle to please
by believing (and memorizing) six
(or maybe just two) impossible
things before breakfast.

But on some Saturday mornings,
when the world news is especially grim,
and all authorities clearly have clay feet,
the words float back
. . . for God so loved the world . . .
and
Jesus loves me, this I know . . .

The grownup world of no illusions,
and its own tangle of anxieties,
is not subject to memorized solutions;
it yields only to the authority of love.

Notes

". . . He ascended into heaven . . ."

The biblical stories of the ascension vary significantly. In Matthew, there is no ascension; rather the book ends with the assurance from Jesus, ". . . remember, I am with you always. . . ." The longer, disputed ending of Mark says that after Jesus had spoken to them, he was taken up into heaven and sat down at the right hand of God. Luke says that, after blessing the disciples, he withdrew from them and was carried up into heaven. John ends his recounting with the report that there were ". . . many other things that Jesus did." These things were so numerous that ". . . if every one of them were written down, . . . the world itself could not contain the books that would be written." In Acts, the ascension takes place in full view of all: "as they were watching, he was lifted up, and a cloud took him out of their sight."

So—it happened in full view, it happened out of sight, it is not reported at all, and/or Jesus stayed around and did all those things that would fill the world with books.

Luke Timothy Johnson suggests that the ascension image is a "book end" to the opening statement in which Jesus "came down" from heaven. If Jesus came from God, was in fact one with God, then he must naturally return to God and his return would be just as mysterious as his entry into the world. (41)

Pushing aside the image of "jet pack Jesus" which has always accompanied these passages for me, and reading them metaphorically rather than in any literal way, one can find a kind of balance in the images of descending and ascending that offers a sense of completion.

However, this "other worldly" exit stands in stark contrast to the grimy details of the crucifixion. We swing between images of vulnerable humanity and impervious divinity, reflecting the tension and struggles the bishops faced in defining Jesus and his likeness or relation to God.

Perhaps the best we can do is to know that the disciples who followed him, some more faithfully than others, would likely spend some time gazing into the sky, into the future, trying to hold onto the image of the one who had stirred a fire in their hearts, and in at least one person's memory, promised to be with them always.

Who has not stood
beside that slash in the earth
that will shortly hold
the one you have held dear,
and not found your eyes
drawn up rather than down,
squinting into the bright haze,
searching for that tear
through which has slipped
all your dreams,
remembering the promise,
"I am with you always."

Promises aside,
spirit sometimes proves to be a poor
substitute for flesh—
and when does "always" begin?

Notes

Notes

". . . and is seated at the right hand of the Father . . ."

Since there could be no witness to such an event, were it literally to be the case, this is again metaphorical language that places Jesus in the most important position relative to God—on God's right hand.

This image is one with ancient roots. In Psalm 110:1, we read

"The Lord says to my lord, sit at my right hand . . ."

Psalm 98:1 proclaims: "His right hand and his holy arm have gotten him victory."

And from Isaiah 62:8: "The Lord has sworn by his right hand and his mighty arm."

Like the early TV westerns, where the good guys and bad guys were easily distinguishable by their white hats and black hats, we have associated good and bad, strength and weakness, even graceful and clumsy, with right and left.

The contrast becomes more evident when we recall cliches in common use: "in the right" means being correct; we swear to tell the truth by raising our right hand; the familiar separation of sheep and goats in the gospel of Matthew puts the sheep (the ones who are blessed) on the right hand, and the goats (the ones who are cursed) on the left hand.

The person who feels clumsy on the dance floor speaks of having two left feet, and to go about something in a left-handed way is to be devious or sneaky. In the past children who were born with dominant left handedness were made to switch to their right hand because the left was considered abnormal or inferior. A left handed person often finds that the world is constructed with only right handed people in mind.

All this to say that, across cultures, the right hand has always been the place of honor, so to speak of Jesus on the right hand of God was to give him the ultimate position of strength, a position of "rightness" relative to all others. This might imply that those who followed him could make such a claim as well, creating some of the difficulty in reaching compromise language for the Creed.

One has to wonder if there is a seat on the left, and whose name is on it.

Ecclesiastes cautions us that
"The heart of the wise inclines to the right,
but the heart of the fool to the left." (10:2)

Would that we all walked with a
visible tilt so our inclinations
were clear to the world.

Or would that only
separate us more
sharply than any sheep or goats,
giving the illusion that I could know
who you are from twenty paces.

Let us at least suspend judgment,
get close enough to each other
to see that there is middle ground,
a place that is neither left nor right,
where we can stand together.

Notes

Notes

". . . He will come again in glory . . ."

In the Gospel of Mark, Chapter Thirteen, there is what scholars call a "mini apocalypse," in which we are told about the events of the last days, or end times. The predictions, or warnings—for some threaten significant destruction—are put into the mouth of Jesus as he addresses his disciples. The setting is in Jerusalem, just days before his betrayal and arrest.

Jesus has predicted the destruction of the temple, or the buildings around it (the prediction is voiced in a way that could mean either). His disciples ask, "Tell us, when are those things going to happen, and what will be the sign to indicate when all these things are about to take place? (13:4) After a series of warnings, Jesus declares,

But in those days, after that tribulation,
the sun will be darkened,
and the moon will not give off her glow,
and the stars will fall from the sky,
and the heavenly forces will be shaken!

And then they will see the Son Of Man
coming on the clouds with
great power and splendor. (13: 24-25)

This scene is echoed in Matthew and Luke, with Mark considered to be the primary source for their versions.

In the book titled, *The Five Gospels: The Search for the Authentic Words of Jesus*, an analysis of the passages leads to a remarkable conclusion: first, the passages are patterned after other apocalyptic passages, such as Daniel, and second, none of the statements can be reliably attributed to Jesus.

A parallel passage is indeed found in Daniel 7: 13-14:

I saw one like a human being
coming with the clouds of heaven . . .
To him was given dominion
and glory and kingship . . .

And what of this question about whether the words do indeed come from Jesus? The attribution is questioned because the sayings "reflect detailed knowledge of events that took place—or ideas that were current—*after* Jesus' death . . ." (42)

One understanding of these writings, and indeed, even the line included in the Creed, is the hope that people had in the midst of persecution that they would be rescued, that life would get better, and that those who persecuted them would be punished. This is a statement of hope, not of fact or prediction.

Jesus on a white horse—

the ultimate rescuer when
the world is coming apart,
the old ways are cast aside,
and all you hold dear is destroyed,
when people you depended on
have turned away,
mocked you,
when the center does not hold.

Jesus on a white horse—

some dreams are ageless.
Little children, grow up.

Notes

Notes

". . . to judge the living and the dead . . ."

In the late 1980's I had the opportunity to pastor a small, rural Methodist church north of Chicago. It was my first church, and I was their first woman pastor—and not even Methodist. All they could afford was a part-time salary, but that worked for me. I came to love them, and they returned the favor. The church was dominated by several families who were, for the most part, welcoming and supportive. Only one family raised objections, and ultimately left the church. The objection was not that I was a woman, or even that I wasn't Methodist, but that I talked too much about love and not enough about sin and guilt.

That couple would perhaps have been more comfortable in the kind of church that Philip Gulley describes in his book, *If The Church Were Christian: Rediscovering the Values of Jesus,* He speaks of his experiences with churches that promote guilt, and he says of this kind of church, "were one determined to damage someone's life, I could imagine few things more destructive than regular exposure to some churches. Guilt is their weapon of choice. Guilt for being born into sin. Guilt for experiencing unavoidable human passions. Guilt for not believing with sufficient zeal. Guilt for questioning settled beliefs. Guilt for doubting . . ." (43)

The fourth century writers of the Creed did not hesitate to judge each other, and torture was not beyond them in pursuing their goals. In their disagreements over the words of the Creed, they excommunicated each other, spied on each other, intimidated, brutalized—in defining Jesus, they lost his values.

The early church had gone through desperate times, and some of its members came to the Council with the scars of torture still upon them. They carried within them the ancient yet overriding wish for punishment for those who had persecuted them. They voiced their accusations against each other in inflated and incendiary terms. They would judge someone not just to be the wrong kind of Christian, but also to be a despicable, immoral person.

Their methods were neither subtle nor moderated by compassion. And while our methods today may seem so mild by comparison as to be inconsequential, they still take a toll on our spiritual self, and our relationship to the Holy. The hymns we sing, the prayers we speak, the table around which we gather—all can deliver a message of guilt cloaked in grace.

If we could truly say this line of the Creed—*to judge the living and the dead*—and mean by it that judgment was indeed God's prerogative, if we could get out of that business ourselves, then we might find it possible to trust that the God who judges us finally, is the God who loves us most fully.

For years,
I can't say quite how many,
I lingered on the edge of the church,
convinced that if they really knew me,
I would not be welcome.

Then I happened upon a church
that held me close,
that would not let me go,
until my heart began to heal.

The tears came each Sunday
as their acceptance washed over me,
erasing the scars of past judgments
from the righteous, from myself,
from the God I thought I knew,
and loving me into grace.

Notes

Notes

"... and his kingdom will have no end ..."

The world of the Creed was a world of kings and emperors. These rulers could be beneficent, or they could turn and impose laws, order property seized, and have lives ended. They were undisputedly in charge of the empire or the kingdom—until they were overthrown and someone else was in charge.

The years in which the Creed was established were in some ways remarkably stable because the empire was unified under one ruler, Constantine. But when Constantine died, his three sons fought each other and the world to gain supremacy, and unity was lost. The people who lived through repeated turmoil naturally wished for peace—and, not finding it in their earthly rulers, they expressed their longing for "a kingdom with no end" that had God as its ruler. Jesus, having brought God near to them, would surely usher in a new reign—a different kind of reign, and one which would have no end.

Though the language of kingdom might speak powerfully to a fourth century citizen, our contemporary associations with it have more to do with encrusted tradition, carefully preserved, *or* repressive dictators with a cruel streak. Some defend continued use of the image because of its place in our tradition, and because of the contrast it offers to earthly kingdoms. It is preserved as well because of resistance to change and the unsettling impact of disturbing familiar images.

But that turmoil would be a small price to pay for the release from patterns of thought and practice detrimental to both women and men. Elizabeth Johnson declares that "the symbol of God functions. It is never neutral in its effects, but expresses and molds a community's bedrock convictions and actions. . . . It [is] piercingly clear that the practice of naming God exclusively in the image of powerful men has at least three pernicious effects."

The first is that, because it offers no alternatives, it is more likely to be taken literally. Second, these dominant male images have functioned to justify patriarchy in church and society. Third, exclusively male language suggests that women are somehow less like God. "Such language thus robs women of the dignity that would accrue if the gracious reality of God were addressed in their own womanly image and likeness." (44)

Johnson also argues that "naming toward God with female metaphors releases divine mystery from its age-old patriarchal cage so that God can be truly God—incomprehensible source, sustaining power, . . . holy Wisdom, indwelling spirit, the ground of being, . . . the holy mystery that surrounds and supports the world." (45)

A soft, hesitant voice came from the back
of the meeting room. "I'd like to share something—
it's something I wrote—I don't know if it would be
helpful or not . . ."
"Please do."
"It's a new doxology . . . it goes like this.
Praise God from whom all blessings flow,
whose womb gave birth to all we know,
who draws us close to her warm breast,
for nurture, love, and perfect rest."

Women and men, we all sat silent.
Someone said, "Amen," and the meeting ended.
As we rose to our feet, women quickly gathered
in a circle to surround the soft-voiced woman.
"Say that again—I want to get the words down—

say it again—and again—and again.

Notes

The focus of the Creed now turned to the Holy Spirit. If One plus One equals One was hard to explain, it became even more difficult when One plus One plus One was still equal to One. The challenge loomed again of finding language that would describe an aspect of God that was not subordinate to God the Father. Basil of Caesarea, who became known simply as Basil the Great, was quoted as saying, *"of the wise men among ourselves, some have conceived of him [the Holy Spirit] as an activity, some as a creature, some as God, and some have been uncertain which to call him . . . And therefore they neither worship him nor treat him with dishonor, but take up a neutral position.* (46)

The continuing efforts to clarify the nature of and relationships between God the Father, God the Son, and God the Holy Spirit stumbled at the complexity, and Basil's answer ". . . *was to declare that what was common to the Three and what was distinctive among them lay beyond speech and comprehension and therefore beyond either analysis or conceptualization.* (47)

For some today, the Doctrine of the Trinity is still central to the Christian faith, while others pass over it more lightly, falling silent at that portion of the Creed, and rejoining with the words "and in one holy catholic . . ." A respected minister preached a series of sermons on the Trinity, saying it was one of the worst pieces of theology every foisted on the Christian church.

Christian theologians, however, continue to offer a variety of images to capture this elusive concept and Elizabeth Johnson has gathered together some of the proposals:

Karl Barth speaks of God the Revealer, the Revelation, and the Revealedness;

Gordon Kaufman "imagines divine absoluteness, divine humaneness, and divine presence . . ."

Paul Tillich speaks of creative power, saving love, and ecstatic transformation;

Langdon Gilkey speaks of God as divine being, divine logos, and divine love;

Peter Hodgson offers the configuration of the one (Father) who loves (Son) in freedom (Spirit);

Sallie McFague interprets the one God as Mother, Lover, and Friend;

Letty Russell conceives of the Trinity as Creator, Liberator, and Advocate.

". . . Whatever the categories used, the terms seek to express a livingness in God who is beyond, with, and within the world and its history. . . . [The] task is to express the inexhaustible fullness of the mystery of the living God, a fullness for which no one expression is ever totally adequate." (48)

Invited to write a prayer expressing the fullness of God in inclusive language, the parishoners of an Anglican church in Canada composed this prayer for Christmas day:

"Maker of this earth our home,
You sweep the heavens with your starry skirt of night,
and polish the eastern sky to bring light to the new day.
Come to us in the birth of the infant Christ,
that we may discover the fullness of your redemption
throughout the universe;
Mother and Child of Peace bound by the Spirit of Love,
One-in-Three forever. Amen." (49)

Notes

Notes

". . . we believe in the Holy Spirit, the Lord, the giver of life . . ."

The Creed which the bishops revealed in June of 325 A.D. gave short shrift to the Holy Spirit. The closing line simply said, "And in the Holy Spirit" and was separated from the "We believe . . ." introductory words by the almost tortuous definitions of the relationship between the Father and the Son.

It was not until 381 A.D. that the bishops, meeting in yet another council in Constantinople, revised and extended the Nicene Creed to include more nearly the lines we recite today which include a belief in

> "the Holy Spirit, the Lord and Life-giver,
> Who proceeds from the Father, Who with
> Father and Son is together worshiped and together glorified." (50)

Whether the language is Hebrew, Latin or Greek, the root terms for the word "spirit" relate to wind, breath, or breathing. Thus the "wind from God" which moved over the waters of creation, and the "violent wind" which rushed through the room on the day of Pentecost, were both understood to be expressions of the Holy Spirit—"Spirit" because, while it gave life to the physical, was itself not physical, and "Holy" to point to its source, which was God.

How would it change the experience of saying this line if it read instead: "We believe in the Holy Breath . . . the giver of life . . ." ? Standing in our orderly rows in the pews, we are caught between the squalling gasp of air that fills tiny lungs for the first time, and the slow, softly rattling breath that we breathe for the last time. On our journey from one to the other, we rely upon that steady and mostly silent, automatic process by which we renew our bodies from moment to moment.

Without spirit, without breath—we cannot live. Even if we question its source, we cannot question its necessity.

Making a distinction that is more theological than physical, we can say that breath gives us life, but "Spirit" enlivens us. We have all known people who we might call "dispirited," meaning depressed, despondent, pessimistic, just as we have known people who we describe as "spirited,: meaning lively, engaging, maybe even opinionated and passionate.

When the bishops attempted to define the third party of the Trinity, perhaps all they needed to do—all we need to do—is take a deep breath.

Sometimes the best word
about God
is silence,
broken only by
the sound of breath,
rippling in laughter,
anguished in tears,
steady in the
focus of thought,
emptying in despair,
shrill at first gasp,
soft at last gasp.

Breathe on me, breath of God,
and enliven me until my last breath.

Notes

Notes

"... who proceeds from the Father *and the Son* ..."

According to Luke Timothy Johnson, author of *The Creed*, the phrase, "and the Son," put things "over the top" as far as the eastern church was concerned, and was the final catalyst for the schism between Catholic and Orthodox Christians in 1054. He notes that this short statement's "ability to create controversy is the more remarkable, since few Christians today have any idea what it means, or why anyone would care about it." (51)

Part of the complaint was theological, but a significant part was also political. The western church added the phrase without the participation of and over the objections of the eastern church, and the interminable dispute has been as much over process as content. Johnson describes it thus: "Here we have a great and bitter battle, all the more savage because it is between family members and over such a minor point. . . . Here we see the unholy alliance between belief and power politics, supporting the suspicion that all belief is simply a matter of power and politics." (52)

Johnson concludes his commentary with a remembrance of Paul's injunction about injuring other believers by our actions. Paul's example is about food: "if food is a cause of my brother's falling, I will never eat meat (I Cor 8:13). Then Johnson pledges, "If my fellow Christian is offended by *filioque* [and the Son], then I have no need to ever say it again." (53) If only that criterion was applied to all the language we use about God!

An examination of the Creed and all the brutal power politics that were the context for its formation can open for us the question: Which is more important—finding the correct words to describe God, or finding the courage and clarity to live into reality the image of God as reflected by the life of Jesus? Words have the power to shape our perceptions of the world, and of ourselves, but they can also divert us from the direct experience of what is vital in our lives. Thomas Aquinas, famous theologian and prolific writer of the 13th century, said toward the end of his life, ". . . all that I have written seems to be like straw compared to those things . . . that have been revealed to me." (54)

Here we face intersecting and seemingly incompatible truths: whenever we speak of God in a way that is meaningful to us, we risk offending someone else whose experience is different. Whenever we risk speaking of God in a way that for us captures some essence of truth, we, and others, will look back at it and declare it to be "straw." So we recognize that all our words are simply stammerings, no matter how eloquently delivered, and we recognize that sometimes it is best to stand silent before the mystery that is beyond all understanding.

One plus One,
both derivatives of One,
when added to One,
still equal One.

It's a different mathematics,
this calculus of the infinite,
with an equation beyond solution,
and a graph defined by the order
of random stars,
whose light draws us to the
clear night sky,
where wonder makes
all calculations cease.

Notes

Notes

". . . with the Father and the Son he is worshiped and glorified . . ."

With the Holy Spirit established as equal to the Father and the Son, via the preceding statement, the writers of the Creed move on to the logical conclusion: the Holy Spirit deserves the same worship and glorification given to the Father and the Son.

Without debating that point, it is interesting to turn to another related question: Is worship and glorification the appropriate response to any or all members of the Trinity?

Worship is defined as reverence and/or adoration, deriving from an Old English term meaning *"recognize the worth of."* We usually think of worship as that time of songs and prayers and sermons, a time when scripture is read, sermons preached, and people are gathered around a common table. Without minimizing the value of these experiences, it seems true to say that if this is our only worship time, then no matter how piously we participate, we have failed to *"recognize the worth of"*, we have failed to worship Jesus, and by corollary, God and the Holy Spirit.

Again referring to Philip Gulley's book, *What if the Church Were Christian*, we find his assessment that ". . . the church's worship of Jesus is something he would not have favored. Further, this tendency has had profound consequences, not all of them beneficial. One consequence has been our tendency to value right thinking above right acting . . ." Other consequences include the encouragement of a prideful stance which asserts that belief in "our" God and Jesus is the only way to salvation, and with this, an exclusivity that undermines the values that Jesus actually lived and taught. (55)

Gulley maintains that Jesus was not about his own glorification, and by extension, we might say that God the Father and God the Holy Spirit are less interested in proper worship than in faithful living. Jesus "... argued for humility, modesty, and putting others before self. ... Instead of accepting [this interpretation], the church made Jesus God, interpreting his life in ways he likely didn't intend, convincing itself that his way of living was so remarkable as to only be possible for him." (56)

When we also "worship and glorify" the Holy Spirit, we fall into the same dilemma. We admire the work of the Spirit from afar, without acknowledging the power we have to enliven, to enrich, to stimulate thought, to make a life of faith that is engaged in worship—recognizing worth—every day, each hour.

The first invitation was to "... believe in the good news ..."
that the kingdom of God had come near.

The second was to "Follow me ..."
over dirt roads, into the hills, into danger,
to bring food, healing, hope,
to reveal that the kingdom of God was here,
for hungry, hurting people.

How did it become all about believing,
all about me,
all about my salvation ...
all about the hereafter,
when the hungry, hurting people
still need food, healing, and hope?

The first invitation depends on our
response to the second.

Notes

Notes

". . . he has spoken through the prophets . . ."

This closing line of confession about the Holy Spirit puts the divine accent on the prophet's speech, throughout the Old Testament as well as the New Testament. The question that comes to mind, however, is whether or not God's prophetic voice has been withdrawn from us, indeed, whether all the prophets belong to the past, rather than to the present.

What would a prophet say today? How would we recognize the Spirit speaking a prophetic word?

Listen for what you hear in these words.

"It's time to face questions for which we have no answers, to address problems for which there may be no solutions. We have to accept the radical uncertainty of our lives, yet meet the challenges that life puts in front of us." (57)

"God is not a mystery but rather another name for mystery—for the vast unexplainable mystery of the world around as we swirl among those billions of stars . . ." (58)

"People in the United States live with an abundance of most everything—except meaning." (59)

"All these years later, the way many of us are doing church is broken and we know it, even if we do not know what to do about it. We proclaim the priesthood of all believers while we continue living with hierarchical clergy, liturgy, and architecture. We follow a Lord who challenged the religious and political institutions of his time while we fund and defend our own. We speak and sing of divine transformation while we do everything in our power to maintain equilibrium. If redeeming things continue to happen to us in spite of these deep contradictions in our life together, then I think that is because God is faithful even when we are not." (60)

". . . choosing to believe one way or the other has nothing to do with how things might really be. We cannot solve not-knowing by believing." (61)

"Worship in the future will be marked . . . by the self-conscious awareness that all of us are or can be God bearers and life givers and that our deepest religious task is to give ourselves away." (62)

"We do not lack for prophetic voices—just the ears to hear them, the heart to heed their call. . . ."

It's a dangerous question to ask:

What now?
What next?
What shall I do with my life?
What am I to say? To whom?

You can't mean that.
Not really . . .
Can we talk . . .
How about if I just volunteer a little more?
You want me to do what??

Notes

Notes

"... we believe in one holy and catholic apostolic church ..."

How have we come from a rag-tag group of men, hiding out in fear, with women who seemed oblivious to danger slipping out the door and back again with food? How have we left behind house churches where communion flowed seamlessly from a shared meal, and blessing was on everyone's lips? How have we moved from the tent-maker with a word from God, to the flower guild, the altar guild, the speaker system, and the professional choir?

In her book, *Leaving Church*, Barbara Brown Taylor describes the experience of moving from pulpit to pew and then to her front porch.

Where Mother Church is concerned, those who stray furthest not only forfeit her protection; they may also be shunned as heretics by those who stay home. . . . Early on, . . . a wide variety of people who all called themselves Christian understood the Christ in a wide variety of ways. . . . For almost three centuries, these choices existed in wild disarray. Then the emperor Constantine, in his imperial wisdom, understood that a faith with no center would never anchor his crumbling empire. So he called all the bishops together, fed them lunch, and asked them to say something definitive about the nature of God in Christ. . . . When the bishops finished crafting a central confession of Christian faith, those who did not choose this option became known as heretics.

In my closet I have a T-shirt with many of their names on it . . . Matthew Fox, Hans Kung, Meister Eckhart, Joan of Arc, . . . Origen, Jesus. All of these people made unauthorized choices in their love of God. . . . Some of them died for their disobedience while others were locked in their rooms. . . . Many of them are spiritual heroes now. At least one of them is revered as the Son of God, but none of them got where they were going without passing through the wilderness first. (63)

Christians still understand the Christ in a wide variety of ways. The only "catholic' or universal aspect of the church in all its expressions is the hope of finding just that—hope—within each other, within ourselves, within the Christ who loiters in the hallway, unrecognized, but waiting, listening.

*The visible church is all the people who get together
from time to time in God's name.
Anyone can find out who they are by going to look.*

*The invisible church is all the people who serve
as God's hands and feet in the world.
Nobody can find out who they are except God.*

*Think of them as two circles.
The optimist says they are concentric.
The pessimist says they don't even touch.
The realist says they occasionally overlap.* (64)

Notes

Notes

"... we acknowledge one baptism for the forgiveness of sins ..."

The request was, I knew, a strange one, and would have to be reviewed by the Bishop of that conference. Several elderly members of this white-washed rural Methodist church wanted me to "re-baptize" them. When I asked why, they explained that they had been baptized as infants, and now, as adults, they wanted to experience, to remember, their baptism. They were quite clear, also, that they wanted to be immersed, not sprinkled. The Bishop gave the nod, with a "don't tell anyone" caution, and we proceeded on one summer Sunday evening to "re-baptize" several faithful Christians, in an above ground, slippery swimming pool owned by one of the members. I don't know if their hopes for an enriching spiritual experience were realized; for myself, a great deal of attention was devoted to gripping the rubber bottom of the pool with my toes so I did not spontaneously join them in the "re-baptizing" experience.

The idea of a second, or even third or fourth, baptism would not have been as unusual in the rural South as it was in this somewhat restrained Mid-west farm land. Baptists, at least some brands of them, were given to baptizing freely, assuming one had a recurring need for repentance and could not get too much of a good thing.

The choice of words in the Creed is interesting—*one baptism for the forgiveness of sins*—considering that the offer from John the Baptist was to be baptized with water for *repentance*, The bishops would surely have known the implications of the Greek term for repentance—it meant that one had a change of mind—as well as the implications of the Greek word for baptism—that it was a ritual of consecration, just as the bread and wine are consecrated for the Eucharist.

There was nothing magical, or even "holy", about the process of being plunged into water while certain words were being repeated. The "holy" part came before—when the person seeking baptism felt a change within, when they were willing to turn from the path they were on, when they were ready to dedicate themselves to a new way of life. The ritual was a public acknowledgment of such, as well as an opportunity for the witnesses to recall and affirm their own baptism and pledge companionship for those who emerged dripping and shivering.

The idea that the ritual of baptism itself could accomplish forgiveness of sins would lead us, like the emperor Constantine, to postpone our baptism until we were near death. That way one could be assured of a clean slate at the time of judgment without the necessity of changing one's way of life beforehand.

Some churches interpret the tradition with an emphasis on consecration—these will offer baptism for infants—while others give more weight to repentance, and offer baptism only to those mature enough to affirm that "change of mind" that reflects repentance and opens the door to forgiveness.

Squalling infant, dressed in heirloom white,
Awkward teenager, pressured by parents,
Sunday school teachers and revival preachers,
adults, compliant or contemplative,
sprinkled or immersed,
young, old, in-between.
Is it for our own sake—our own forgiveness—
our own ultimate fate?
Or do we seek this consecration
to help us live
for God's sake?

Notes

Notes

". . . we look for the resurrection of the dead . . ."

It is my guess that each time this line is repeated, at least some of those present will find their mind going, however briefly, to the memory of a beloved person no longer alive, and feel the flickering hope that there is yet to be a reunion, that somehow, somewhere, someday, they will be joined in a familiar embrace.

At his scolding best, Paul writes to the church at Corinth on the subject:

But someone will ask, "How are the dead raised? With what kind of body do they come?" Fool! What you sow does not come to life unless it dies. And as for what you sow, you do not sow the body that is to be, but a bare seed, perhaps of wheat or some other grain. . . . What I am saying, brothers and sisters is this: flesh and blood cannot inherit the kingdom of God, nor does the perishable inherit the imperishable. . . . Listen, I will tell you a mystery. . . . (I Cor 15: 35-51)

But despite all his telling, it remains a mystery, a mystery that many have gone to great lengths to solve. Paul could not have imagined the technology and medical skill that attend our dying and permit a kind of living death, or even a resuscitation after death.

Is it a trick of the mind, a phenomenon of brain chemistry? For some who are revived or resuscitated, there are the reported experiences of an out-of-body reality, when the "perishable" is left behind and the "imperishable" continues to observe. There is, for others, the apparent if invisible, "imperishable" presence of important loved ones in the days and hours prior to death. And for us still moored in the "perishable" flesh, there is the dreaming moment that reunites us with people we have loved in a fashion so real that we wake ourselves reaching for an embrace.

Perhaps the impenetrable mystery of all this is behind the choice of words for this line of the Creed—not "We believe" or even "We acknowledge," but rather, "We look for. . . ."

We hope. We long for. All of which testifies to our capacity, God-given and just as mysterious, to love each other deeply, faithfully, through and beyond death.

The reference book,
with its long columns
of print too small for aging eyes,
says that "resurrection"
in a literal sense means "standing up."

Each morning, then,
is a resurrection.

A resurrection out of
oblivion or dreams,
a resurrection into
one more day before
the mystery that even
St. Paul cannot unravel
enfolds me.

Notes

Notes

"*. . . and the life of the world to come.*"

In an intriguing fantasy about what life would be like as an "imperishable" spirit, freed from the prosaic life of the flesh, Scott Peck speculates about the transition from flesh to spirit, from the life of this world to the life of the world to come. It's title, *In Heaven as on Earth*, gives away his premise. We have all known some version of the characters he peoples his story with— the overweight, depressed office manager with the chocolate bars stashed in her desk, a driven CEO who longs for less pressure and more leisure at the same time that he is working another deal. (65)

In Peck's story, each of the characters has died, and is profoundly disappointed in what they have encountered in the afterlife. Though they are now "imperishable" spirits, they still feel the burdens of the flesh— the office manager still experiences herself as obese, and is indignant that heaven has not blessed her with a trim physique. The CEO finds himself in a barrel with other people where he must constantly strive to stay on top or else he will suffocate or be crushed.

There are guides in this transition space to help them understand that their life in the spirit dimension will only change for the better when they have changed their conception of themselves.

If we say these words about "the life of the world to come" with the assumption that God is busy designing an ideal setting for us, we may find ourselves trailing the relics of this world with us, now and in any future that lies ahead.

This life is the only one we know for sure that we are given—it is this life that we have consecrated through our baptism, it is this world, this creation that nurtures us and deserves nurture from us in return, it is this embodied, incarnated, human self, in all its particularities, that allows us to experience the world, and binds us to each other through our common needs.

"The life of the world to come" is not a fantasy, not an escape, not somewhere "over the rainbow" or "beyond the clouds." It is a life and a world that we co-create each day, in the choices we make, in our willingness to look in the mirror of other's eyes and see ourselves, in the comfort we offer to those in distress—all in all, in our willingness to follow the ways of Christ as well as to confess our belief about Christ.

When the sun rises
through tattered, rosy curtains
hung on bare branches
and stitched together with bird tracks
I believe the life of the world
to come is here and now,
begging to be lived.

Notes

Notes

Amen.

So be it. Let it be as you have said.

That's how the Creed is concluded. Is that what you mean to say? Does it speak your faith, touch your heart? Is it beautiful or just archaic? Does it capture some ultimate truths, or is it a political argument? Are there advantages or disadvantages to having an established creed?

It is a good thing to feel connected to a community, and the recitation of a Creed, voices blending together, builds a sense of belonging. The Creed carries our history, for good or ill, reminds us of where we have been, and points us to the future. For those who need it to function that way, it can serve as an "end point," a definition of their fath that marks the path clearly. For others it serves as a point of beginning or departure, inviting them to engage with the faith tradition and explore its far corners.

But those who have questions or concerns about the content of the Creed can feel isolated in the middle of a communal experience. If the same creed is a recurring part of worship, it can become "automatic," and meaningless for some. Any creed is, by virtue of its human construction, a partial statement that has stringent limits on its capacity to capture all the nuances of faith. An established creed can become petrified and unyielding to new theological insights or expressions.

Two very different people who have written books about creeds are Luke Timothy Johnson, former Benedictine monk, and Joan Chittister, present Benedictine sister. At the close of a 300+ page book on the Nicene Creed, Johnson makes an extended case for the Creed. His first endorsement is based on its simplicity and clarity: "*The Creed is clear, it is not ambiguous or complicated. It can be understood and affirmed by children as well as by adults."* (66) But in the closing pages of his book, he recommends that *"Christians should learn the origin and functions of the creed. . . . They should come to grips with the creed's sometimes strange language and ask, "Do we actually know what we are saying when we say this?"* (67)

Joan Chittister's response to the creed is more lyrical. In her closing pages she says, *"The Creed does not define God. The Creed posits God. The Creed confronts us with the concept of faith and requires us to face the fact that God is as good an answer as we have to anything."* (68)

Simple? Complex? As good an answer as we have to anything?

Perhaps all of the above. But wherever we come down, we must face the reality that our words matter. When we say the word "God," we are giving a name to what is ultimate in our lives. When we attempt to talk about that which is ultimate, we cannot speak in the abstract, but rather must talk about life and the world, about our deepest needs, problems, and fears, about what we love and for what we hope.

With words we construct our world and our reality. Words like almighty, salvation, heaven, power, death, judge, kingdom, worship, baptism, forgiveness, resurrection—they are all powerful words that we weave together to construct the fabric of our life.

Listen to the words. Explore them. Pay attention to how you feel when you say them. Be silent, and listen to them said by other voices. Try different ones. Feel their power to shape your experience and your faith.

And finally, face the silence - the mystery—the limits of all our words to name the holy.

"For everything there is a season . . ." including ". . . a time to keep silence . . ."

Amen.

Finding Your Own Words . . .

"You can say that Christ died for our sins. You may say that the Father has forgiven us because Christ has done for us what we ought to have done. You may say that we are washed in the blood of the Lamb. You may say that Christ has defeated death. They are all true. If any of them do not appeal to you, leave it alone and get on with the formula that does. And, whatever you do, do not start quarreling with other people because they use a different formula from yours."

C. S. Lewis (69)

The Nicene Creed may say all you need to say, or it may not hold what is true for you at all. It's language may leave you in awe or in frustration. It's "formula" may make perfect sense or be offensive to your understanding of God's relation to humankind. It may have attained an almost biblical integrity or it may be one voice among many from Christian history.

It can be a challenge, in the face of established tradition, to find your own expression, your own "formula" that operates, perhaps even unknown, for you. Sometimes we can say, not what we believe to be true, but only what we hope is true. Whatever you choose to say, or not say, in worship, listen to other voices of faith, and then find your own.

I believe that we have been created by God
and invited to live life fully, fearlessly and with grateful hearts.

I believe that we have been called into community
with those nearby and all of humanity and
asked to treat one another with compassion and respect.

I believe that we are caretakers of this world
and are challenged to live in it with joy and reverence.

I believe in the long history of people
who have been touched so deeply by God's presence
and who have been our teachers and our models,
most especially Jesus of Nazareth.

And I believe that all of us, today and tomorrow,
may rest secure in the love of God.

An Advent Faith

They say you showed your face in the face of a child,
in the face of a man,
who, when you looked in his face,
made you see your own as if for the first time.

They say alleluias sounded when you were born,
and echo still in December nights
so that hearing them
you sense hope as if for the first time.

They say that travelers brought you gifts,
and so the swirl of gifts begins,
in bright papers and curling ribbons,
trying to package joy
so that you discover it anew as if for the first time.

They say we must learn to wait,
to wait for your coming;
that you come again to our hearts
with joy, with hope, with that face
that opens all of life.

They say . . .

And I wait . . .
In darkness, in stillness
for that first star
to light the way.

I believe in God, who
when I am lost, seeks me out,
when I come home, broken and hungry, celebrates my return,
when I am anxious, comforts me,
when I am defeated, works the leaven of the
spirit into my soul,
when I am grieved, sustains me,
when I choose darkness over light, forgives me,
when I am unlovely, loves me.

I believe in God, who
when I am creative, creates anew with me,
when I am glad, rejoices with me,
when I have questions, blesses my seeking,
when I wake with wonder, opens my eyes to new vistas,
when I reach out with love, overflows my heart.
I believe in God, who
calls us together in the name of Christ,
and bids us love each other as we are loved.

For Further Reflection . . .

At the heart of all the questions to ponder, there is the primary conviction that **metaphors matter**. As the Contemporary Theology class, whose interests and discussions play a major part in this book, began its study and discussion of The Nicene Creed, we stumbled at the opening words—*We believe in God the Father. . . .* There was no argument about the metaphorical nature of these words. We had studied the historical contexts of the gospels, the history of their formation, the subsequent development of doctrines about the divinity of Jesus and the Trinity, the gradual encrustation of the church with liturgical language, the process of literalization of this language and a hundred other topics that would rattle anyone of a more traditional perspective. We were, after all, the Contemporary Theology class, accustomed to walking the theological edge and exploring the latest theological ideas.

We were prepared to pass quickly through the *God the Father . . .* to *Maker of Heaven and earth . . .* when a comment brought us to a halt. In response to a brief commentary on the obvious gender issues contained in the " Father" image, (brief because we had covered this topic more than once in the past), one woman said, almost under her breath, "I like the "father" reference. It reminds me of my father, and I could always count on him to be helpful and supportive. He was just never critical." At least one other woman echoed similar sentiments, and it quickly became apparent that, for those who had loving, reliable, earthly fathers, the metaphor of a "Father" who was also God, could, on most days, carry warm associations. Rather than feeling diminished or excluded, these women in particular felt their faith allied with positive experiences of a real, human father.

As we talked more about the impact of our experiences in relationships and families and how they give shape and meaning to the metaphors of our lives, a previous similar conversation about the geography of faith came to mind, in which we had noted the realities of the different metaphors and images that were meaningful for those who lived in the barren stretches of the northern plains contrasted with those who came to the faith in a lush, tropical setting. The loving human father, in whatever setting, created an environment for physical, emotional, intellectual and spiritual development which paralleled the tropical one, with the equivalent of plenty of rain and sun and good soil in which to grow.

But for those whose experience of "father" was harsh, unpredictable, unreliable, even abusive or violent, the opening address to "God the Father . . ." stood, not as an invitation to warm associations, but as a recall of an environment filled with solitude, struggle, conflict, and even pain—an environment in which one could grow, yes, but growth that incorporated isolation, confusion, stress and anxiety. "Father" became, for these people, men and women alike, a stumbling block to the remainder of the Creed. It not only disconnected them from the acknowledgment of the holy, but also created a sense of disconnect from those standing next to them in the pews, whose murmuring voices reciting in union this affirmation "God the Father" seemed to create a sense of community they could not join.

The conversation of the class moved on to note that other tangible factors had an impact on the choice and development of metaphors—gender, of course, health, education, extent of exposure to other cultures—not only did all these generate different metaphors, they also created different meanings for the same metaphor.

It was not possible to have that conversation without a review of the frequently heard argument for retaining the language of this Creed in particular, as well as other standardized liturgical formulas: "*On any Sunday, in any church* (of certain denominations), *I can know what to expect, I will say the same words I have always said, and hear the same words I have always heard.*" In other words, I will be comforted by the familiar; I will feel connected both to my community at home, and to the community in which I stand in the moment. The power of the familiar, the need for reassurance through continuity—these all take precedence over the reality that for many, at least in our class, the liturgy and the hymns bespeak a theology they have long ago discarded. Because the metaphors employed do not, at minimum, stir painful associations, they can stand and kneel and sit, absorbing the melody of the hymns, the murmuring voices, the flickering candles, the gilt of the vestments, the bite of the wine on their tongue as they kneel by their neighbor.

But there are others, and their number is not small, who have been sensitized to the power of words by their experiences of how a word can inflict a wound, end a relationship, depress a spirit. They hear each word, and feel the sting of exclusion as they fall silent at all the "he's " and "his", at the "God the Father . . .", at "Father, Son and Holy Spirit." What may be mere hints to some of a substitutionary atonement theology trumpets to them, and can create tightness in the chest, a seeking out of the closest exit, and a scanning of the bulletin to see when an escape can be most quietly pursued.

Metaphors matter. They matter not only to the individual, with all their idiosyncrasies of perception, experience, belief, and history. They matter also to the community, how it is formed, how it relates within itself, and how it extends itself to the larger community of which it is a part.

So what is the liturgical writer, the prayer book editor, the committee on worship, to do? How to balance the retention of the ancient words of the faith, with the reality that they both nurture AND wound the faithful of today? For those who have lived through it, it is said that little arouses so much passion as the revision of treasured liturgy and hymns.

One would almost think that the entire deconstruction of the faith is being advocated. And deconstruction there surely is—for to delve into a metaphor can mean being left with a handful of mist, which evaporates even as one strives to cling to it. But deconstruction offers more than mist. With courage, and the willingness to live with uncertainty, it can offer the endowment of ancient metaphors with deeper meaning, and the enrichment of worship and the language of faith with new metaphors that remind us we cannot capture the sacred with our limited vocabularies.

Yes, it is true that well-worn words, handled with care and respect over centuries, can carry the echoes of the early days of the faith. But it is only by delving into those words that we can hear, not only the reverberations of a crystalizing faith, but the agonized cries of people upon whom those words were imposed by terrible and bloody means. It is in their memory, in respect of their suffering, that we must constantly appraise our metaphors and how we use them.

And yes, it is true, that freshly minted metaphors, with the shine still on them, can grab our attention, can rob us of our assumptions and our sureness, can revise our understandings of who we are, of who, or even what, or whether, God is.

When a question is posed from the audience, as it frequently is at gatherings of progressive Christians, about the issues of language and metaphors, a distillation of the proffered answers points the questioner to tradition, to a different understanding of the words based on contextual study, to a silent, mental "translation" process that expands the scope of the prayer book language. So the reference to "the kingdom which will have no end" becomes "the unending reign of God". To understand that this "kingdom without end" was, in its formative time, fashioned as a repudiation of other earthly kingdoms, does bring a different dimension of meaning to it. But it leaves in place many of the attributes of the "kingdoms" we still build today. Refusing to change the words we speak leaves in place the "sins" of hierarchy, inequalities of all kinds, and servitude based on economics, to mention a few.

While it is true that any metaphor, old or new, will strike the ear, the mind, and the heart of each worshiper in a different way, it is also true that the same metaphors, used over and over, tend to establish themselves as THE metaphors, with the implication that they convey the truth of who God is and who we are in relation to that God. Using Berger's terms, cited in the opening pages, the metaphors become so powerfully legitimated that we are completely alienated from the insight that these words are human creations, and that we have the capacity to continue creating. This tyranny of traditional metaphors makes it difficult to step outside the world of the prayer book, or book of worship, or hymnal, makes it difficult for some to find the God they need to sustain them when life takes non-traditional or unexpected turns.

To say that "metaphors matter" is not to argue for a wholesale clean-out, bargain basement sale of cherished traditional forms. It is to argue for balance, for room to be surprised by God and by what we may find in our own hearts.

Sources

1. Peter Berger, *The Sacred Canopy: Elements of a Sociological Theory of Religion* (New York: Anchor Books, 1969), 3–51.
2. Berger, *The Sacred Canopy,* 9.
3. Gordon Kaufman, *An Essay on Theological Method* (Missoula, Montana: Scholars Press, 1979), 6.
4. Kaufman, *An Essay on Theological Method,* 5.
5. W.H.C. Frend, *The Early Church* (Minneapolis: Fortress Press, 1982), 148.
6. Richard Rubenstein, *When Jesus Became God* (Orlando: Harcourt, Inc., 1999), 104.
7. Robert Jensen, *All My Bones Shake* (Brooklyn, NY: Soft Skull Press, 2009), 3.
8. Luke Timothy Johnson, *The Creed: What Christians Believe and Why it Matters* (New York: Doubleday, 2003), 11.
9. W.H.C. Frend, *The Early Church,*148.
10. Frend, *The Early Church,* 10.
11. Sandy Sasso, *In God's Name* (Woodstock, Vermont: Jewish Lights Publishing, 1994).
12. Nick Greene, "Biography of Giordano Bruno," accessed August 6, 2011. http://space.about.com/cs/astronomyhistory/a/giordanobruno.htm.
13. http://www.blupete.com/Literature/Biographies/Science/Copernicus.htm
14. Barbara Brown Taylor, *The Luminous Web: Essays on Science and Religion* (Boston, Massachusetts: Cowley Publications, 2000), 87.
15. Frend, *The Early Church,* 55–57.
16. Andrew Jones, "Physics of the Greeks," accessed August 6, 2011. http://physics.about.com/od/physicshistory/a/Greekphysics.htm.
17. Rubenstein, *When Jesus Became God,* 98.
18. Marcus Borg, *Putting Away Childish Things* (New York: HarperOne, 2010), 327–331.

19. Phillip Jenkins, "Fighting Words," *The Christian Century*, March 23, 2010, 23.

20. Johnson, Luke Timothy, *The Creed: What Christians Believe and Why it Matters*, 119.

21. Mary Cartledge-Hayes, *To Love Delilah* (San Diego, California: LuraMedia, 1990), 83–84.

22. *A New Zealand Book of Prayer*, p. 481.

23. John Shea, *The God Who Fell From Heaven* (Allen, Texas: Thomas More, 1992), 75.

24. "One of us" Lyrics by Eric Bazilian, originally released by Joan Osborne.

25. Http://www.enotes.com/shakespeare-quotes/lady-doth-protest-too-much-methinks

26. Frend, *The Early Church,*151.

27. Rubenstein, *When Jesus Became God*, 115.

28. Rubenstein, *When Jesus Became God*, 149–150.

29. Rubenstein, *When Jesus Became God*, 145–146.

30. Rubenstein, *When Jesus Became God*, 16–17.

31. John McQuiston, *Always We Begin Again* (Harrisburg, Pennsyvania: Morehouse Publishing, 1996), 1.

32. Henry Bettenson and Chris Maunder , editors, *Documents of the Christian Church* (Oxford: University Press, 1999), 27–28.

33. Marianne Micks, *Loving the Questions: An Exploration of the Nicene Creed* (New York: Seabury Classics, 2005), 40.

34. Frances Frank, "Did the woman say?" *Celebrating Women* (Wilton, Connecticut: Women in Theology, 1988)

35. John Dominic Crossan, *The Birth of Christianity* (San Francisco: Harper Collins, 1998), 27–29.

36. Frederick Buechner, *The Faces of Jesus* (New York: Riverwood/Simon and Schuster, 1974), various.

37. Elizabeth Geitz, *Gender and the Nicene Creed* (New York: Church Publishing, 1995), 50.

38. Daniel Bell, "God does not demand blood," *The Christian Century*, February 10, 2009, 22.

39. Bell,"God does not demand blood", 25.

40. http://ww.christianhistorytimeline.com/lives_events/more/canon2.shtml

41. Johnson, *The Creed*, 187.

42. Robert W. Funk,, et al. *The Five Gospels: The Search for the Authentic Words of Jesus* (New York: Macmillan, 1993), 110.

43. Philip Gulley, *What if the Church were Christian: Rediscovering the Values of Jesus* (New York: HarperOne, 2010), 32.

44. Elizabeth Johnson, *Quest for the Living God: Mapping Frontiers in the Theology of God* (New York: Continuum, 2007), 98–99.

45. Johnson, *Quest for the Living God,* 99.

46. Rubenstein, *When Jesus became God,* 206.

47. Rubenstein, *When Jesus became God,* 209.

48. Johnson, *Quest for the Living God,* 219–221.

49. Johnson, *Quest for the Living God,* 107.

50. Rubenstein, *When Jesus became God,* 222.

51. Johnson, *The Creed,* 228.

52. Johnson, *The Creed,* 231.

53. Johnson, *The Creed,* 231.

54. Fred Sanders, *Thomas Aquinas' Big Pile of Straw,* dated December 6, 2010. Http://www.scriptoriumdaily.com/2010/12/06/thomas-aquinas

55. Gulley, *What if the Church were Christian,*17.

56. Gulley, *What if the Church were Christian,* 25.

57. Jensen, *All My Bones Shake,* 8.

58. Jensen, *All My Bones Shake,* 48.

59. Jensen, *All My Bones Shake,* 119.

60. Barbara Brown Taylor, *Leaving Church* (San Francisco: Harper, 2006), 220.

61. Marcus Borg, *The God We Never Knew* (San Francisco: Harper, 1997), 175.

62. John Shelby Spong, *Why Christianity Must Change or Die* (San Francisco: Harper, 1998), 187.

63. Taylor, *Leaving Church,* 176.

64. Frederick Buechner, *Wishful Thinking: A Theological ABC* (New York: Harper & Row, 1973), 15.

65. Scott Peck, *In Heaven As on Earth* (New York: Hyperion, 1996).

66. Johnson, *The Creed,* 301.

67. Johnson, *The Creed,* 323.

68. Joan Chittister, *In Search of Belief* (Liguori, Missouri: Liguori/Triumph: 2006), 198.

69. C. S. Lewis, *Mere Christianity* (New York: Macmillan, 1972), 157.

Bibliography

Bazilian, Eric. "One of Us," originally released by Joan Osborne.

Bell, Daniel M. "God does not demand blood," *Christian Century* (2/10/09): 22 26.

Berger, Peter. *The Sacred Canopy: Elements of a Sociological Theory of Religion.* New York: Anchor Books, 1969.

Bettenson, Henry and Chris Maunder, editors.. *Documents of the Christian Church.* Oxford: University Press, 1999.

Borg, Marcus. *The God We Never Knew.* San Francisco: Harper, 1997.

Borg, Marcus. *Putting Away Childish Things.* New York: HarperOne, 2010.

Buechner, Frederick. *The Faces of Jesus.* New York: Riverwood/Simon and Schuster, 1974.

Buechner, Frederick. *Wishful Thinking: A Theological ABC.* New York: Harper & Row, 1973.

Cartledge-Hayes, Mary. *To Love Delilah.* San Diego, California: LuraMedia, 1990.

Chittister, Joan. *In Search of Belief.* Liguori, Missouri: Liguori/Triumph, 2006.

Church of the Province of New Zealand. *A New Zealand Prayer Book.* New Zealand: Collins, 1989.

Crossan, John Dominic. *The Birth of Christianity.* San Francisco: Harper Collins, 1998.

Frank, Frances. "Did the woman say?" *Celebrating Women.* Wilton, Connecticut: Women in Theology, 1986.

Frend, W. H. C. *The Early Church.* Minneapolis: Fortress Press, 1982.

Funk, Robert W., Roy W. Hoover, and the Jesus Seminar. *The Five Gospels: The Search for the*

Authentic Words of Jesus. New York: Macmillan, 1993.

Geitz, Elizabeth. *Gender and the Nicene Creed.* New York: Church Publishing, 1995.

Gulley, Philip. *If the Church were Christian: Rediscovering the Values of Jesus.* New York: Harper One, 2010.

Jenkins, Philip. "Fighting Words," *Christian Century* (3/23/10), 22–25.

Jensen, Robert. *All My Bones Shake.* Brooklyn, New York: Soft Skull Press, 2009.

Johnson, Elizabeth. *Quest for the Living God: Mapping Frontiers in the Theology of God.* New York: Continuum, 2007.

Johnson, Luke Timothy. *The Creed: What Christians Believe and Why It Matters.* New York: Doubleday, 2003.

Kaufman, Gordon. *An Essay on Theological Method.* Missoula, Montana: Scholars Press, 1979.

Lewis, C. S. *Mere Christianity.* New York: Macmillan, 1972.

McQuiston, John. *Always We Begin Again: The Benedictine Way of Living.* Harrisburg, Pennsylvania: Morehouse Publishing, 1996.

Micks, Marianne. *Loving the Questions: An Exploration of the Nicene Creed.* New York: Seabury Classics, 2005.

Peck, Scott. *In Heaven as on Earth: A Vision of the Afterlife.* New York: Hyperion, 1996.

Rubenstein, Richard. *When Jesus Became God.* Orlando, Florida: Harcourt Inc., 1999.

Sasso, Sandy. *In God's Name.* Woodstock, Vermont: Jewish Lights Publishing, 1994.

Shea, John. *The God Who Fell From Heaven.* Allen, Texas: Thomas More: 1992.

Spong, John Shelby. *Why Christianity Must Change or Die.* San Francisco: Harper, 1998.

Taylor, Barbara Brown. *The Luminous Web: Essays on Science and Religion.* Boston, Massachusetts: Cowley Publications, 2000.

Taylor, Barbara Brown. *Leaving Church.* San Francisco: Harper, 2006.

In Your Own Words

Actual human speech about God . . . is not abstract logical talk about an 'ultimate limit', but rather talk about life and the world, about our deepest problems, about catastrophe and triumph, about human misery and human glory. (1)

If you recall the concepts formulated by Peter Berger, and summarized in the Preface of this book, then you will be aware that you are entering into a creative, **constructive** period. You may find that many of your initial thoughts will be shaped by concepts and terms which, through years of use, have achieved an objective or given quality. To walk outside this familiar territory will likely feel unsettling. Inviting creative speech about God, and then experiencing that speech as part of worship, is disconcerting partly because it means taking responsibility for formulating your own definitions of the phenomenon we call "God." This is a term laden with meaning, guarded by the church and the clergy in the name of tradition, as well as by many in the congregation in the interests of continuity and comfort.

Entering this process also means risking a certain degree of vulnerability. You will find that you are called to speak, not about "abstract, logical" thoughts and ideas, as Gordon Kaufman puts it, but about "life and the world, about our deepest problems," indeed, about those things which matter most to you. The questions always arise: "Will my words be adequate?" "Will others ridicule what I think or say?"

Because this exploration has that "unsettling" quality, it may be best done in a small group, where trust has been built, and where questions, observations, metaphors, interpretations, and insights can all be shared and explored in safety—and you find out over and over that you are not alone in your exploration.

There are a few commitments that are necessary to create and maintain an effective small group experience, especially one that involves the vulnerability of open conversation and theological reflection. Therefore, every person in the group must agree to observe the following group guidelines:

- *Confidentiality*—this means that what is said in the group is not repeated outside the group in a way that the source can be identified. Example: It is not appropriate to say to anyone, even your spouse or partner, "You'll never believe what Bill said in group!" You can say, if you wish to process something outside of group, "An interesting perspective was shared in group," or, "I heard a point of view I had never considered before."

- *Openness*—each person in the group agrees to express their thoughts, reactions, and feelings in the group, and to be a full participant in the group

- *Acceptance*—Respect and acceptance are to be granted for each participant; you may ask questions of someone in order to more deeply understand their perspective or experience, but you may not critique or demean the views of others

- *Commitment*—each member of the group commits to be present at every gathering for the agreed upon period. Any necessary absences should be communicated to the group in advance if possible.

- *Involvement*—each member of the group agrees to keep up with readings and other assignments or projects that are a part of the group experience

- *Support*—Individually and collectively, the group must strive to offer support for the fullest exploration of this Mystery we seek to affirm, of the language that structures our thoughts, and the traditions that have shaped us.

- *Responsibility*—Each member of the group agrees to take their turn leading (or co-leading) the discussion. Discussion assignments should be made during the first gathering of the group. If the group determines that sharing a meal or refreshments as part of their time together enhances the experience of hospitality and connection, then the responsibilities for that will be equally shared.

The following sections assume that each person is familiar with The Nicene Creed, and has read the reflections as suggested. It is also helpful to be familiar with some of the current books and dvd's about Jesus and the context of his life and ministry. There are some excellent resources listed in the bibliography, and a variety of materials can be accessed through Faithandreason.org and Livingthequestions.com.

The goal for this experience is NOT to arrive at a new creedal statement, but to explore and become aware of your personal belief system, to assess how those beliefs are impacting your life, to find your place relative to the community of faith where you may belong, and to discover those spiritual practices or manners of expression that sustain you in your life of faith.

This is best done in community, and the hope is that through sharing this experience with others, supportive spiritual connections will be formed, and the foundation laid for further explorations together.

Session One: God

(We believe in one God . . .)

A TIME OF GATHERING AND REFLECTION

Begin with a brief period of silence.

Read the following aloud and allow time for reflection.

One of the central contemporary theological problems is that many of the traditional concepts and categories—including especially "God"—no longer seem related to our actual experience. (2)

Share first impressions and thoughts about this reading.

Read aloud the following, allowing opportunity for comments and discussion as the reading proceeds.

So what comes to mind? The ceiling of the Sistine Chapel and the life giving touch of a finger tip? The aloof bearded man on the judgment throne? The creator of all that is taking a moment to roll something sparkling between gnarled fingers, and then tossing it like a star pitcher into the distance, where it explodes and blooms into all the corners of the sky? Is it the God who got sick of us and opened the flood gates to wash away the failed experiment, giving the chance for a "re-do?" Or is it the God who bears us up on eagles' wings, sustaining and protecting us? For all the metaphors that we employ, we must ask: is God in any way person-like? Does God have a personality or character?

Certainly in our pervasive disobedience of the OT injunction to make no graven images, it has been widespread custom to represent God as a very old, and therefore wise, male human being. However, before we begin characterizing God, it might be best to acknowledge that we KNOW, in the same way that we know our best friend or our spouse, *nothing* directly about God. In the throes of intense experience, you might have the sense of being sustained by something "other;" in peaceful, quiet moments you might feel a connection to a "presence." It is just as possible to feel overwhelmed by "absence," by a deep awareness of separateness. The content of your experiences, as well as how you interpret them, are influenced by your setting, your life experiences, your relationships. These same influences operate as you make your constructions, your creation of God. What is true for you may not be true for the next person. As we will see in examining particular metaphorical language for God and Jesus, your interpretations will be unique to your life.

Rather than thinking of these different visions as competing visions, with one true and the other false or invalid, with the necessity for you or anyone to fight for a particular vision to be the prevailing one, we can remember the old adage about the blind men trying to describe an elephant just by feeling of him. Their reports depended entirely on what part of the elephant they happened to encounter, and how they interpreted what they felt, never having seen the whole picture. Even pooling their impressions could only give them a limited grasp of the elephant, but at least it was more productive than arguing about whether the elephant was more like a tree trunk or more like a flexible hose.

Annie Dillard gives a compelling description of our limitations in her collection of essays *Teaching a Stone to Talk*. In a section titled "Assorted Wildlife," she writes: "I like insects for their stupidity. A paper wasp . . . is fumbling at the stained-glass window on my right. I saw the same sight in the same spot last Sunday. Pssst! Idiot! Sweetheart! Go around by the door! I hope we seem as endearingly stupid to God—bumbling down into lamps, running half-wit across the floor, banging for days at the hinge of an opened door. I hope so. It does not seem likely." (3)

And so, having read through the Nicene Creed in some detail, with curiosity and humility allow it to serve as a template or beginning point for the Creed you actually live.

The Nicene Creed begins with the words, "We believe in one God . . ." Deconstructing this phrase, and then reconstructing it, we might ask questions like:

- Who is the audience for this statement of faith or theological reflection? God? Friends? Family? Yourself?

- Should the statements be ABOUT God, framed to speak what we believe or hope for in relation to God, as in "We believe in God . . ." or

- Should the statements be addressed TO God, in admiration or acknowledgment, as in "We believe in YOU, O God . . ."

- What difference does this make as you think about writing about your faith?

- Should a statement about God be communal or individual? How would you address or take into account the diversity of beliefs in any group of people who gathered for worship or study?

- What is important about declaring that there is "one God?" Do we live this as a truth, or do we have multiple other "gods?" Does the Christian concept of "Trinity" introduce multiple gods for you? Does that doctrine have meaning for you? If so, what does it mean? Does it really represent something true about God, or is it trying to capture some qualities that we attribute to God?

- The word "God" itself trails multiple meanings as it slips off our tongues in hymns and prayers. There are several ways to approach that word: to begin with a basic definition; to attribute qualities or characteristics; to associate certain actions, past, present and future; to speculate on how or if God interacts with the world today; to wonder what this phenomenon we call "God" wants from us, if anything?

When your discussion has been concluded, or the agreed upon time has elapsed, begin to move toward closing.

RETURN TO THE SILENCE. LET ALL THAT YOU HAVE HEARD, ALL THAT YOU HAVE THOUGHT, SINK INTO A QUIET PLACE WITHIN YOURSELF. LET THE SILENCE GROW.

IN A BRIEF SENTENCE OR PHRASE, SPEAK YOUR CONCERNS, QUESTIONS, AND CELEBRATIONS INTO THE SILENCE.

DEPART WITH A RESPONSIVE BLESSING:

Leader: There is one source of creation

People: hidden from our view by time and space.

Leader: There is one source of creation

People: not hidden from our hearts;

Leader: there is one source of creation

People: which grateful hearts turn to

Leader: in wonder, in openness, in hope

People: that creation will stir in us

All: and we will be one with the source of creation.
           Amen.

Notes

Notes

Session Two: God

(. . . The Father, the Almighty . . .)

A TIME OF GATHERING AND REFLECTION

Begin with a brief period of silence.

Read the following aloud and allow time for reflection.

We no longer can settle theological issues by appeal to the authority of scripture or tradition. We must now undertake the much more difficult and hazardous task of deliberately and self-consciously constructing our concept of a God who is an adequate and meaningful object of devotion and center for the orientation of human life. (4)

Share first impressions and thoughts about this reading

Now read aloud the following, allowing opportunity for comments and discussion as the reading proceeds.

- The title "Father" is a human term denoting both a role and a relationship. Is this an acceptable or meaningful title for you, or would you prefer something more inclusive or more neutral? What would be some alternative titles? Try reading through the Book of Common Prayer or a hymnal, changing all the parental references to "Mother" and all the "he's" to " her's". How does that change your image of God? Your image of yourself in relation to God?

- What about nonhuman, nongendered titles such as the Sacred, or Holy Mystery, or Source of Wisdom, Creator, etc. What impact do such titles for God have on your image of God and God's accessibility?

- What are the implications of giving God the title of "Almighty?" Does that concept conflict with how you see the world operating—that is, bad things continue to happen, both by accident and by human intent. Does God's power to intervene have limits? Are those limits chosen? What if God is not "Almighty?:" Who's running the show? Is anyone? If we acknowledge our own free will in determining at least some aspects of our lives, how does that interact with God's power?

- What do you believe about God's function or role in bringing all that is into being? What do we do with our inability to conceptualize beyond "the big bang?"

- In his book, *All My Bones Shake*, Robert Jensen says that "God is not a mystery but rather another name for mystery—for the vast, unexplainable mystery of the world around us as we swirl among those billions of stars, as well as the mystery inside us as those billions of cells interact to create us." (5)

- How would you address such a mystery?

When the discussion has been concluded, or the agreed upon time has elapsed, begin to move toward closing.

RETURN TO THE SILENCE. LET ALL THAT YOU HAVE HEARD, ALL THAT YOU HAVE THOUGHT, SINK INTO A QUIET PLACE WITHIN YOURSELF. LET THE SILENCE GROW.

IN A BRIEF SENTENCE OR PHRASE, SPEAK YOUR CONCERNS, QUESTIONS, AND CELEBRATIONS INTO THE SILENCE.

DEPART WITH A RESPONSIVE BLESSING:

Leader: The name is "mystery."

People: The name is "silence."

Leader: The name is "creator."

People: The name is "beauty."

Leader: The name is "terror."

People: The name is "hope."

Leader: The name is "fear."

People: The name is "love."

ALL: The name is mystery, silence, creator, beauty, terror, hope, fear, love—and the greatest of these is love.

Amen.

Notes

Session Three: God

(. . . Maker of heaven and earth, of all that is, seen and unseen . . .)

A TIME OF GATHERING AND REFLECTION

Begin with a brief period of silence.

Read the following aloud and allow time for reflection.

"God must be conceived in some specific way, as some sort of reality or other . . . The concept of God . . . is always constructed with the aid of models drawn from ordinary experience. . . . Perhaps the predominant material notion that has been used to develop the conception of God is that drawn from the human experience of creation. . . ." (6)

Share first impressions and thoughts about this reading

This begins the reflection upon and formulation of your own expression of faith. Read aloud the following, allowing opportunity for comments, discussion and writing as the process continues.

- Take some time now to begin writing: first, a list of characteristics you might attribute to God; second, the qualities of relationship you experience with God and how that experience happens. Then, in just a few lines, write a draft of a statement, a prayer, a hymn, an affirmation, or a poem that incorporates some of these characteristics and qualities.

- Imagine what you have written being repeated or read in worship. Would you change anything?

Read aloud the prayer below, and talk about the questions which follow. Any further ideas on editing or refining your own statement? Remember that no single statement can be comprehensive; limit your construction, knowing that you can always expand upon what you write at any one time.

FLINGING STONES

Silent God, we quiet ourselves for a whisper from you.
Invisible God, we strain our eyes for a glimpse of you.

Silent, invisible God,
we fashion words and skip them out across the spaces
like stones flung across a smooth and shimmering lake—
sharp words of anxiety and fear,
smooth words of hope and gratitude.

Invisible, silent God,
from here we cannot tell if these words
so flung into space
sink finally into the depth of your being
or skip endlessly out into widening pools of nothingness.

But fling them we must—in continual hope
that we will hear a splash—see a ripple.

So—silent, invisible God, I sling a small smooth stone
of gratitude for quiet pools of peace, for friends, for green trees hinting
    at scarlet.

And a sharp, broken stone of anxiety, of fear, of shame
for all the hurt and suffering that we create in this world of plenty.
Rob us of our illusions. Let us be changed.

Hear our prayer. Amen.

Discuss the following:

What qualities are attributed to God?
What various feelings are contained within the relationship with God?
Which is stronger—belief or hope?

To gain another perspective, read aloud the following. It may be helpful to
read it more than once. A decidedly playful tenor of relationship with God
is expressed in this poem/prayer/affirmation by Kaylin Haught titled *God
says Yes to Me.*

I asked God if it was okay to be
melodramatic
and she said yes
I asked her if it was okay to be short
and she said it sure is
I asked her if I could wear nail polish
or not wear nail polish
and she said honey
she calls me that sometimes
she said you can do just exactly what
you want to
Thanks God I said
and is it even okay if I don't paragraph

my letters
Sweetcakes God said
who knows where she picked that up
what I'm telling you is
Yes Yes Yes

The metaphors are wildly different, but they vividly convey a relationship of grace. How do you find yourself responding to this affirmation of faith?

If you are participating in a mixed gender group, listen for the different ways in which women and men respond. What is your own response to a God characterized as "she?"

Look again at what you have written. Do you want to add anything—edit anything out?

If you are working in a group, begin reading and listening to each other's statements. If you are working by yourself, let what you have written sit for a few days. Then look back at it and see how it sounds to you. Again imagine reading it in worship, or having it published in your church newsletter. Would you change anything? Why? How do you imagine people would respond?

Were it to be shared either in worship or via a newsletter, would you rather it be anonymous? If so, why?

RETURN TO THE SILENCE. LET ALL THAT YOU HAVE HEARD, ALL THAT YOU HAVE THOUGHT, ALL THAT YOU HAVE WRITTEN, SINK INTO A QUIET PLACE WITHIN YOURSELF. LET THE SILENCE GROW.

IN A BRIEF SENTENCE OR PHRASE, SPEAK YOUR CONCERNS, QUESTIONS, AND CELEBRATIONS INTO THE SILENCE.

DEPART WITH A RESPONSIVE BLESSING:

Leader: Listen! Listen to each other!

People: Your god is different from mine.

Leader: Learn! Learn from each other!

People: I never thought of god that way.

Leader: Accept! Accept each other!

People: I can say "yes" to your God.
          Can you say "yes" to my God?

ALL: Sweetcakes—what God says to all of us is
          Yes Yes Yes.

          Amen.

Notes

Session Four: Jesus

(We believe in one Lord, Jesus Christ, the only Son of God,
eternally begotten of the Father, God from God, Light from Light,
true God from true God, begotten, not made, of one Being with the Father,
Through him all things were made)

A TIME OF GATHERING AND REFLECTION

Begin with a brief period of silence.

Read the following aloud and allow time for reflection.

*". . . the original mistake made at Nicaea . . . was to assume that doctrinal differences among Christians were not **that** important, that they did not reflect serious divisions of class, culture, and moral values within the community. . . ."* (7)

Share first impressions and thoughts about this reading

Now read aloud the following, allowing opportunity for comments and discussion as the reading proceeds.

Immediately, with the opening lines of the Creed, its authors began to make a claim for Jesus that was among the most hotly debated, as well as the initiator of bloodshed, because it was a direct challenge to the vested powers of Rome and the divine lineage claimed by various Roman leaders.

The Bishops who gathered in Nicaea were themselves not all of one mind about Jesus, but they did seem to share a crucial perspective: Jesus was no ordinary man, but rather in some way, which they tried to define with tortuous accuracy, uniquely related to God.

Those perspectives sprang from questions like "Was he the Son of God? A rural peasant? An itinerant preacher? A learned teacher? A mystical healer? Leader of a Jewish revolution?"

With multiple metaphors, the Bishops tried to answer the question definitively: Jesus was fully divine AND fully human. Their first focus was on the "divine" aspects of Jesus—he was "the ONLY Son of God . . ." and had been for all eternity. A central component of the controversy about these statements was whether or not there should be a hint of subordination— after all, most sons at least start out subordinate to their fathers, and mature gradually into equality. But others would have none of this—Jesus was as much God as God and always had been.

The arguments no doubt reflected more about the Bishops, and who they would like to define as worthy of worship and endowed with a saving power, then they did about Jesus himself. They were making a competing claim to the established powers of the day, one which they could not prove except by repetition.

To the extent that Jesus is central to your faith experience, what qualities do you find essential to attribute to him? Do you think of him as divine? As an extraordinary human?

What difference does it make?

Some people make a distinction between the Jesus of history and the Christ of faith. Modern scholarship has yielded much about the context or, as Dom Crossan would put it, the "matrix" into which Jesus was born—a small, rural village, suffering economically under Roman exploitation of the local resources and with little power to resist Roman oppression.

Many contemporary theologians, at least those with the security or the courage to speak what they believe, would say that the Jesus of history was born into a world with increasing domination and exploitation of working class people. Seeing this and responding out of his convictions and compassion, he pursued the path of nonviolent resistance to the powerful people who dominated their world.

Clearly something about the way he lived and related to people, the way in which he spoke truths that people could recognize, perhaps the way in which he eschewed personal power to dominate, yet spoke with the power of integrity and compassion—all these qualities combined to form a very memorable man, whose impact remained alive in his community even after his death.

- What does it mean to "believe" in him?

- When you see the distinctions made between the Jesus of history and the Christ of faith, do you feel torn about his true identity? Are the two roles necessarily incompatible?

- How would you answer Jesus's question, "And who do you say that I am?"

- In the Creed, the Bishops outlined what was important to them about Jesus—"*God from God, Light from Light, true God from true God . . .*" What is important to you about Jesus's identity? What meaning does the Christ of faith have for you?

- What does it mean to you to question, or even discard, the formula for salvation—"accepting Jesus Christ as your Lord and personal savior," "being born again," believing that Jesus died on the cross for your sins. Do you remember when you first heard this? How does it feel to challenge it? What keeps you engaged with the stories, the rituals, the traditions?

RETURN TO THE SILENCE. LET ALL THAT YOU HAVE HEARD, ALL THAT YOU HAVE THOUGHT, SINK INTO A QUIET PLACE WITHIN YOURSELF. LET THE SILENCE GROW.

IN A BRIEF SENTENCE OR PHRASE, SPEAK YOUR CONCERNS, QUESTIONS, AND CELEBRATIONS INTO THE SILENCE.

DEPART WITH A RESPONSIVE BLESSING:

Leader: It was a long, long time ago

People: In a different place and time

Leader: but the power of compassion

People: the power of acceptance

Leader: the power of gentleness

People: the power of grace

ALL: keep us seeking to find and to follow.

Notes

Notes

Session Five: Jesus

"For us and our salvation he came down from heaven:
by the power of the Holy Spirit
he became incarnate from the Virgin Mary . . .
and was made man."

A TIME OF GATHERING AND REFLECTION

Begin with a brief period of silence.

Read the following aloud and allow time for reflection.

. . . the gospels are not straightforward historical documents but are the developing traditions of the early Christian movement put into written form in the last third of the first century. . . . (8)

. . . it is very important to a correct . . . understanding of the creed to note that . . . "became truly human" is . . . a more accurate translation of the original Greek text. . . . it is Jesus' humanity that is of significance in the incarnation, not his maleness . . . (9)

Share first impressions and thoughts about these readings.

Read aloud the following, allowing opportunity for comments and discussion as the reading proceeds.

Now the Bishops move from declaring *who* Jesus is, to defining *how* and *why* Jesus is. The *why* comes first. *"For us and our salvation. . . ."* If we presume that "us" includes ALL of us—a generous presumption considering the assembly it came from—then the question is, "What does salvation mean?" From whom—or what—do we need saving? What would that look like?

The Bishops do not elaborate in the Creed, but the default definition of "salvation" usually relates to being saved from eternal damnation and consignment to hell. For some people, maybe a lot of people, this is still their default definition, and it is the underlying fear related to this that energizes them to get up, get dressed, and go to church to sit through one more service on a Sunday morning.

Evangelical pastor Rob Bell has recently drawn critical attention by raising questions about judgment and hell and our ultimate fate. To question that default definition is to question the structure of the faith universe. If hell is removed as a consequence for bad or evil behaviors, then what will keep us in line? Will we all just get "out of control?" So we are left to ponder these questions:

- What can we discover about the meaning of "salvation" as used in the Creed? What does it mean to you?

- What are we being saved from? Or to?

Stories of a "special" birth were, in the first century, a common way of attributing an equally "special" status to a person. For some believers, the virgin birth is a crucial element of the Christian faith. Without it, Jesus is just like any other human being, and therefore, unable to deliver the necessary salvation.

- Think of the last time you saw a new born baby—one who entered this world in the ordinary way—conceived through a physical act—nurtured within a physical body—born through physical exertion—

with blood circulating and breath enlivening from the first moments. Could this be Jesus? Could this blood-streaked squalling infant somehow be the "word" of God? Does it matter if it's a boy or a girl?

- Does the conception and birth of Jesus have to take place in an extraordinary way, or is every birth an extraordinary expression of life? If we hear the stories of Jesus' birth as metaphorical rather than literal, what other metaphors would convey the extraordinary possibilities in his life, or in any life?

- The season of Advent is a time in particular when we contemplate this birth and all it came to mean. In the poem which follows, all of Advent becomes a metaphor for the life it announces.

An Advent Faith—They say . . .

They say you showed your face in the face of a child,
in the face of a man,
who, when you looked in his face
made you see your own face
as if for the first time.

They say alleluias sounded when you were born,
and echo still in December nights
so that hearing them
you sense hope
as if for the first time.

They say that travelers brought you gifts,
and so the swirl of gifts begins,
in bright papers and swirling ribbons,

trying to package joy
so that you discover it anew
as if for the first time.

They say we must learn to wait,
to wait for your coming,
that you come again to our hearts
with joy, with hope, with that face
that opens all of life.

They say . . .

And I wait . . .
In darkness, in stillness
for that first star
to light the way.

Do you find yourself waiting for, hoping for, some kind of revelation about all this? When do you experience the reality or the power of something beyond you, or as Marcus Borg would put it, the "more?" Does the mundane have the power to communicate the extraordinary? What qualities do you associate with the "extraordinary?" Beauty, simplicity, complexity, endurance, laughter, song . . . ?

RETURN TO THE SILENCE. LET ALL THAT YOU HAVE HEARD, ALL THAT YOU HAVE THOUGHT, SINK INTO A QUIET PLACE WITHIN YOURSELF. LET THE SILENCE GROW.

IN A BRIEF SENTENCE OR PHRASE, SPEAK YOUR CONCERNS, QUESTIONS, AND CELEBRATIONS INTO THE SILENCE.

DEPART WITH A RESPONSIVE BLESSING:

Leader: In the silence, we wait.

People: We wait for meaning, for truth to be revealed.

Leader: In the darkness, we wait.

People: We wait for purpose, for hope to be born.

Leader: In the dawning light, we wait.

ALL: And then we turn to see each other,
           to find meaning, truth, purpose and hope,
           to see the extraordinary in the most ordinary,
           to know saving grace in an open heart,
           to bear that grace into the world.

Notes

Session Six: Jesus

"For our sake he was crucified under Pontius Pilate;
he suffered death and was buried.
On the third day he rose again in accordance with the scriptures;;
he ascended into heaven and is seated at the right hand of the Father.
He will come again in glory to judge the living and the dead,
and his kingdom will have no end."

A TIME OF GATHERING AND REFLECTION

Begin with a brief period of silence.

Read the following aloud and allow time for reflection.

". . . The language of original sin and atonement has emanated from Christian circles for so long that it has achieved the status of a sacred mantra. This means that it cannot be questioned . . . Yet, upon closer inspection, these sacred concepts involve us in . . . a theistic understanding of God . . . , [and] a magical view of Jesus that violates our mind. . . . (10)

Share first impressions and thoughts about these readings.

Read aloud the following, allowing opportunity for comments and discussion as the reading proceeds.

It was in the ensuing years after the death of Jesus that the purpose of his life and death was reshaped and redefined. In a religious context where the sacrifice of animals to please or appease God was the norm, to say that Jesus was the "once and for all" sacrifice was to defy the religious authorities, while to name him "King of the Jews" flaunted the political elite. The attribution of a substitutionary purpose to his death would come still later, with theological reasoning becoming continually more complex and philosophical. The focus shifted from the communal to the personal, from a powerfully different way of resisting Roman oppression to the more individually focused concern about salvation—being saved out of what was a difficult world to live in, being reassured that God, through Jesus, was looking out for you.

- What purpose do you think this language serves?

- What do you think is the function of Jesus as an icon, a figure of devotion?

- From what are we being saved—fear, anxiety, loneliness, loss, death?

Heinz Kohut, founder of the psychodynamic theory of self psychology, maintains that "disintegration anxiety" is "the deepest anxiety man can experience." (11) In his understanding, even hatred, or perhaps condemnation for sin, can preserve a sense of humanness because it recognizes the individual's existence. What is most threatening is "exposure to the coldness, the indifference of the nonhuman, the nonempathically responding world." (12) Lacking the presence of a responsive environment, we may employ our imaginations to supply the needed acknowledgment or empathy—hence we characterize Jesus and God as loving, as present, as sustaining, as forgiving, as just and righteous, as free of the failings which beset us, as powerful, as humble—as whoever and whatever will shore up our sense of self in a nonresponsive or arbitrary world.

In the formulas that we devise to manage these existential anxieties, we can lose the central message of the stories which have survived the years—

to love God, however conceived, and YOUR NEIGHBOR as your self—to bring justice to our relationships, whether communal or personal—to extend compassion and acceptance to the other, even when the other is alien to you.

- What would you add as central to the message of Jesus?

- What concept of Jesus is most reassuring or meaningful to you?

- What fears threaten to creep in if the traditional concepts are dismantled or discarded? What do you lose? What do you gain?

Take some time now to begin writing: first, a list of characteristics you might attribute to Jesus; second, the qualities of relationship you experience with Jesus, if you do, and how that experience happens. Then, in just a few lines, write a draft of a statement, a prayer, a hymn, an affirmation, or a poem that incorporates some of these characteristics and qualities.

- Imagine what you have written being repeated or read in worship. Would you change anything?

Remember that no single statement can be comprehensive; limit your construction, knowing that you can always expand upon what you write at any one time.

- Take turns reading aloud what you have written. What surprises you about what you hear? Do you hear anything that makes you want to revise what you have written?

- Look at the variety of ways in which Jesus has been portrayed in art, either through internet research, (see Jesus at 2000) or through a book like *The Faces of Jesus* by Frederick Buechner. What do the images convey to you? Do they change your perceptions or the way you would describe Jesus?

Below is an acrostic poem from the resources of *Living the Questions*. The first letters of each line spell our "Who do you say that I am?

When years ago you came walking into my
home, bringing
offerings of love, wrapped in
dull images
of gardens and rocks, all serious with crosses on the hillside,
You didn't tell me that I could leap
over all those centuries of creeds and crusades
until I
stood with you cooking fish on
a fire beside a sea with fishing boats and
young people ready for
the differences that they
had tasted once
and wished would come again
to
inspire, disturb,
accompany, heal, bless, and
make new. Or perhaps you did and I just never heard you the way I do now.

Or try a shorter word, like "Bible," and see what can happen. Some examples are below.

But how could I know,
imagination aside, that you were the

bread of life,
lingering by the shore, the smell of fish on your hands, being
enough for all.

But you came
ignoring all the distinctions
bringing light and grace
love and hope
enough for all

Beyond the words
Is the Word,
bursting through the limits
laid down across time,
entering all hearts with love.

Because of you
I changed directions
because of you
limits disappeared
exposing horizons to explore.

RETURN TO THE SILENCE. LET ALL THAT YOU HAVE HEARD, ALL THAT YOU HAVE THOUGHT, ALL THAT YOU HAVE WRITTEN, SINK INTO A QUIET PLACE WITHIN YOURSELF. LET THE SILENCE GROW.

IN A BRIEF SENTENCE OR PHRASE, SPEAK YOUR CONCERNS, QUESTIONS, AND CELEBRATIONS INTO THE SILENCE.

DEPART WITH A RESPONSIVE BLESSING:

Leader: Beyond any words,

People: We seek the Word.

Leader: The Word that speaks to our hearts,

People: The Word that opens our hearts to others,

Leader: The Word that cannot be contained on a page,

ALL: The Word we must live into being.

Notes

Notes

Session Seven: All the Rest

We believe in the Holy Spirit, the Lord, the giver of life,
who proceeds from the Father and the Son.
With the Father and the Son he is worshiped and glorified.
He has spoken through the prophets. We believe in one holy catholic and
apostolic church,
we acknowledge one baptism for the forgiveness of sin.
We look for the resurrection of the dead,
and the life of the world to come.

A TIME OF GATHERING AND REFLECTION

Begin with a brief period of silence.

Read the following aloud and allow time for reflection.

Writing of her experience of leaving church, in the book of that name (*Leaving Church: A Memoir of Faith*), Barbara Brown Taylor asks these questions: *"Did the Nicene Creed really cover all the bases of the Christian story? Was the Bible always the word of God?"* and then comes to these new conclusions: *"Freed from defending the faith, I began to revisit what faith really means to one and found that much of the old center did not hold. . . . I had arrived at an understanding of faith that had far more to do with trust than with certainty. I trusted God to be God even if I could not say who God was for sure. . . . I trusted God to hold me and those I loved, in life and death, without giving me one shred of conclusive evidence that it was so."* (13)

Read aloud the following, allowing opportunity for comments and discussion as the reading proceeds.

One gets the feeling that the Bishops, given their charge by the emperor Constantine, and secluded in the surroundings furnished by the Emperor, were much more meticulous in the opening days and weeks—even months—of the Nicene conference. What seemed to occupy most of their time was the identity of Jesus. In these closing lines of the Creed, they moved with relative alacrity through such elements as the Holy Spirit, the church, baptism, forgiveness, sin, and resurrection. Each of these could be, indeed, have been, the subject of whole volumes of work, where they are defined with astonishing certainty—"the Holy Spirit is . . ." or "the church represents. . . ."

We seem to always be about trying to define the undefinable, to capture an experience, a feeling, in words or in a picture. While it is legitimate to try and communicate, through words or symbols or rituals, a significant experience, we tend to take our feeble attempts at describing an experience and make them stand in the place of the experience. We take stories that people wrote and turn them into "sacred" scripture; we take a meal with the closest of friends and turn it into a ritual. We are trying to capture an experience and repeat it, make it available when and where we need it. In so doing, we can lose the essence of the experience that captured our hearts to begin with.

For example, the familiar artistic representation of the Holy Spirit as a white dove descending upon Jesus at his baptism ignores the root of the word "spirit," which in the biblical languages was always associated with "wind" or "breath." The use of such metaphors argues not for a separate being which must be incorporated into a trinitarian Godhead, but for "breath"which is an integral part of God, just as our breath is an integral part of our physical human experience. All of this to say that the Holy Spirit is an elusive concept, as elusive as the dynamic that can enliven a community gathered as "church," as individual as the significance of the ritual we call baptism, as challenging as the process of forgiveness, as persistent as the reality of sin, however defined, and as hopeful—that somehow life will continue to be breathed into us—as the anticipation of resurrection and the life of the world to come.

- Consider which of these elements of the Creed—Holy Spirit, church, baptism, forgiveness, sin, resurrection, the life of the world to come— you would include in a statement of faith.

- Would they be more likely to find a place in a statement of hope?

- What is your favorite ritual or re-enactment within the Christian story? What feeling does it convey to you?

- Can you tell the story of your first communion, your baptism, when you joined a church that felt like home, the first time you attended a funeral?

- If you were telling someone about your faith, would you include any of these elements? What would you say and how would you say it—a statement, a story, a hope, a prayer, a hymn?

- Take some time to write a brief statement about one of these elements. Try using the acrostic structure—each line begins with a letter in the word you choose. For example, If the chosen element is "sin":

Separated, broken,
ignoring the call to love,
negating you and myself all in the same moment.

Take turns reading aloud what you have written. Do you hear anything that surprises you? Would you want to change what you have written? What about reading what you have written in worship?

Are there things you would want to include in an affirmation of faith or hope that have not been addressed? Remember that whatever you include, whatever you have written, is subject to change as you continue your faith journey. What you hear, what you see, what you learn will change you and how you regard your relationship with what is sacred and with others.

WHEN THE READINGS ARE FINISHED, THEN RETURN TO THE SILENCE. LET ALL THAT YOU HAVE HEARD, ALL THAT YOU HAVE THOUGHT, ALL THAT YOU HAVE WRITTEN, SINK INTO A QUIET PLACE WITHIN YOURSELF. LET THE SILENCE GROW.

IN A BRIEF SENTENCE OR PHRASE, SPEAK YOUR CONCERNS, QUESTIONS, AND CELEBRATIONS INTO THE SILENCE.

DEPART WITH A RESPONSIVE BLESSING:

Leader: When the sun rises

People: through tattered, rosy curtains

Leader: hung on bare branches

People: and stitched together with bird tracks

ALL: I believe the life of the world
          to come is here and now,
          begging to be lived. AMEN.

Notes

Notes

Sources

1. Gordon Kaufman, *An Essay on Theological Method* (Missoula, Montana: Scholars Press, 1979), 13.
2. Kaufman, *An Essay on Theological Method,* 7.
3. Annie Dillard, *Teaching a Stone to Talk: Expeditions and Encounters* (New York: Harper & Row, 1982), 41.
4. Kaufman, *An Essay on Theological Method,* 57.
5. Robert Jensen, *All My Bones Shake* (Brooklyn, NY: Soft Skull Press, 2009), 48.
6. Kaufman, *An Essay on Theological Method,* 52–53.
7. Richard Rubenstein, *When Jesus Became God* (Orlando: Harcourt, Inc., 1999), 133.
8. Marcus Borg, *Meeting Jesus Again for the First Time* (San Francisco: Harper, 1994), 20.
9. Elizabeth Geitz, *Gender and the Nicene Creed* (New York: Church Publishing, 1995), 50–51.
10. John Shelby Spong, *Why Christianity Must Change or Die* (San Francisco: Harper. 1998), 85.
11. Heinz Kohut, *How Does Analysis Cure* (Chicago: The University of Chicago Press, 1984), 16.
12. Heinz Kohut, *How Does Analysis Cure?,* 18.
13. Barbara Brown Taylor, *Leaving Church: A Memoir of Faith* (San Francisco: Harper, 2006), 169–170.

Bibliography

Borg, Marcus. *Meeting Jesus Again for the First Time*. San Francisco: Harper. 1994.

Dillard, Annie. *Teaching a Stone to Talk: Expeditions and Encounters*. New York: Harper & Row. 1982.

Geitz, Elizabeth. *Gender and the Nicene Creed*. New York: Church Publishing. 1995.

Jensen, Robert. *All My Bones Shake*. Brooklyn, New York: Soft Skull Press. 2009.

Kaufman, Gordon. *An Essay on Theological Method*. Missoula, Montana: Scholars Press. 1979.

Kohut, Heinz. *How Does Analysis Cure?* Chicago: The University of Chicago Press. 1984.

Rubenstein, Richard. *When Jesus Became God*. Orlando, Florida: Harcourt Inc. 1999.

Spong, John Shelby. *Why Christianity Must Change or Die*. San Francisco: Harper. 1998.

Taylor, Barbara Brown. *Leaving Church*. San Francisco: Harper, 2006.

Other Resources

LivingtheQuestions.com

Faithandreason.org

Foundation for Contemporary Theology, Houston, TX

contemporarytheology.org

What Would Jesus Buy? (Video)

Pray the Devil Back to Hell (Video)